Mindful
Manners

For Sallie, whose exceptional manners spring from a kind and loving heart

&

For Jimmy, whose spirit of love and friendship endures

Inspiring | Educating | Creating | Entertaining

Brimming with creative inspiration, how-to projects, and useful information to enrich your everyday life, Quarto Knows is a favorite destination for those pursuing their interests and passions. Visit our site and dig deeper with our books into your area of interest: Quarto Creates, Quarto Cooks, Quarto Homes, Quarto Lives, Quarto Drives, Quarto Explores, Quarto Gifts, or Quarto Kids.

This edition published in 2019 by Crestline,
an imprint of The Quarto Group
142 West 36th Street, 4th Floor
New York, NY 10018 USA
T (212) 779-4972 F (212) 779-6058
www.QuartoKnows.com

First published in 2017 by Wellfleet Press, an imprint of The Quarto Group,
142 West 36th Street, 4th Floor, New York, NY 10018, USA.

Crestline titles are also available at discount for retail, wholesale, promotional, and bulk purchase. For details, contact the Special Sales Manager by email at specialsales@quarto.com or by mail at The Quarto Group, Attn: Special Sales Manager, 100 Cummings Center Suite 265D, Beverly, MA 01915, USA.

Cover and Interior Design: Ashley Prine, Tandem Books
Additional illustration credits: vertical-stripes border © swiejko/Creative Market, diagonal-stripes borders © solarbird/Shutterstock, tribal-ikat borders © Ann Muse/Shutterstock, fleur-de-lis © Helga Wigandt/Shutterstock, triangle borders © Lumen/Shutterstock, watercolor backgrounds © Norrapat Teapnarin/Shutterstock

10 9 8 7 6 5 4 3 2 1

ISBN: 978-0-7858-3728-2

MIX
Paper from responsible sources
FSC
www.fsc.org   FSC® C008047

Printed in China

Previously published as Etiquette Rules!: A Field Guide to Modern Manners

Mindful Manners

Modern Etiquette
for a Better Life

CRESTLINE

CONTENTS

INTRODUCTION   VI

Chapter 1
YOUR PERSONAL BEST

Prepare for Success 1

Building Your Brand 2

Appearance and Attire 3

First Impressions 3

Clothes Encounters 4

Gauge in Brain
(Formal vs. Informal) 5

Hygiene and Grooming Guide 10

Posture 11

Grammar 11

Swearing and Offensive
Language 11

Time Sensitivity 12

Feedback 13

My Space 13

Wrap Up 13

Chapter 2
PEOPLE SKILLS

Take a Hard Look at
Your Soft Skills 15

Connecting and Building
Rapport 17

Listening Skills 19

Conversational Skills 21

Body Language 23

Handshake and Other
Greetings 24

Introductions Playbook 25

Name Game 30

Networking Etiquette 33

Disability Etiquette 37

Chapter 3
YOUR WORLD

Living with Manners 41

Retail Rudeness 51

Medical Office Manners 57

Etiquette of Worship 58

Parking Lots and Garages 59

Chapter 4
FUN AND FITNESS

Entertainment 61

Health and Fitness 63

Chapter 5
MANNERS HIT
THE ROAD

Getting There 71

Hotel Hospitality 82

Chapter 6
COMMUNICATING COURTESY

Thank-You Notes and Letters 89
Business Letters 90
Words of Condolence 94
Grammar Review 97

Chapter 7
GOING SOCIAL

Cell Phone Courtesy 103
Texting 106
Social Media. 108

Chapter 8
BE OUR GUEST

Invitations 115
Receiving an Invitation 117
Party Playbook 121
Houseguest Handbook. 128
Gifts—General Guidelines 130
Party Protocol. 131

Chapter 9
MANNERS GO TO WORK

Job Interview Etiquette. 139
You're Hired!
    Welcome Aboard 143
Gender-Neutral Courtesy 147

Business Cards—Owner's Manual . . 149
Meetings Manners. 153
EZ Email Etiquette. 157

Chapter 10
DINING DECODED

General Guidelines 163
Tabletop Tour. 168
Dining Styles 173
Restaurant Dining 177
Customer Courtesy 179
Fast-Food Finesse 182
Food-Service Glossary 185

Chapter 11
DOWN THE AISLE

Determine Your Vision. 191
Timeline 192
Save-the-Date
    Announcements 193
Invitations. 194
Ceremony. 204
Reception. 205
Gifts. 209
Thank-You Notes 211

ACKNOWLEDGMENTS   212
INDEX   213
ABOUT THE AUTHOR   216

INTRODUCTION

R udeness is rampant. It is on display when we drive, dine, shop, talk and text, and when we work and play. It has become so prevalent that it is now difficult to define polite behavior. Studies indicate that 70 percent of Americans are disturbed by the lack of courtesy in our society. Many recognize rudeness but are unsure how or if to react. Print, radio, and television journalists, authors, bloggers, and tweeters agree with the general population that civility is sagging and needs a boost. In these pages we will examine *rude* and ways to combat it. A good place to start is within ourselves, doing our part to shore up civility.

Imagine for a moment that there is an app that can ensure that you are

- polished and professional;
- comfortable and confident in new situations;
- able to put others at ease;
- respectful, kind, and considerate;
- invited often; and
- remembered, in a good way.

Raise your hand if you would download it immediately. Who wouldn't? Well, dreams come true! The "app" exists, it's free to all, and it runs on a handy smart device—*you*. It's called *etiquette*, the long-established set of rules and traditions governing manners and courtesy. Yes, that one. I can hear the push back now: "Etiquette is so last century." "Does anyone still pay attention to those rules?" "How can anything so old school be practical today?" I am happy to report that etiquette is alive and well and has evolved to fit the times. Get ready to change your mind-set about manners.

Etiquette today is not about how you hold a teacup. It's a powerful tool that can change your personal and professional life and the lives of those around you. When you know and follow etiquette rules and traditions, you demonstrate respect, you build personal and business relationships more easily, and your life flows more smoothly.

Each of us at one time or another has heard that tiny voice in the back of the brain that asks, "Was my behavior rude or insulting in any way?" "What's the right thing to do in this situation?" "Did I offend my relative/friend/colleague?" To avoid this self-doubt, why not raise your etiquette IQ and always be assured that you won't offend, insult, or disrespect the people in your life. The process involves more than memorizing rules. It requires that you adopt a mind-set in which you think about others and their needs as often as you think about yourself and what you need. Courtesy becomes an integral part of your character, and you don't turn your manners on and off. They are on duty twenty-four seven.

The rules of etiquette can be compared to a common language that all successful people must learn to speak. By reviewing the material contained in this book, you can become fluent in etiquette, and you will become an ambassador of civility. People make choices in their personal and professional lives, and they choose to spend time with people they like and respect, people who show consideration and promote civility.

Can one person change the world? Yes, each of us can have a profound impact on our world and the lives of those around us by being courteous, considerate, and kind.

CHAPTER 1

YOUR PERSONAL BEST

In today's fiercely competitive world, etiquette intelligence is an important tool to add to your arsenal. This knowledge will help you treat others with kindness and respect, improve relationships, radiate confidence, and establish and protect your brand. Long story short, your etiquette IQ makes it possible for you to help others and help yourself at the same time.

In this chapter, we will turn the spotlight on *you*. We'll start by helping you take a personal inventory to determine if you are ready for success or if there's work to be done. You will learn that etiquette IQ is not measured by the number of rules you can memorize; rather, it is how you embrace the tenets of civility by demonstrating courtesy and respect to everyone in your life.

PREPARE FOR SUCCESS

People who are successful and effective in their careers and social circles develop not only an expertise in their field but an overall polish in appearance and demeanor as well. They know how to listen, greet others, make introductions, converse on many subjects, empathize, dine with dignity, and treat all people with respect. By learning and demonstrating etiquette skills, you can increase your level of comfort and success in social and business settings. The polish and self-confidence that result will help you accomplish your goals more quickly and lead a life with fewer bumps in the road.

Your manners are a window into your character and reflect how you feel about yourself, the people in your life, and the world around you. How do your manners measure up? If you are not the polished professional you want to be, then begin today on a course of self-improvement using etiquette as your syllabus.

BUILDING YOUR BRAND

Think of yourself as a salesperson for a product that you want to promote. The product is *you*. Are you ready for the marketplace? Many services and products available today are often so similar that buyers must look for differences in quality and reputation. Take stock of your personal inventory—image, people skills, trust, courtesy, and reliability. Does your inventory measure up to your consumers' expectations, and will it help you to achieve your goals? While etiquette intelligence alone will not ensure success in your personal or professional life, it will help you feel comfortable and confident in a variety of situations and give you an edge over others.

BRAND DEVELOPMENT

Your first assignment in personal brand development is to make a list of ten adjectives relating to your character that you think friends and colleagues use when they describe you. Be honest—it's a self-assessment for your eyes only. Does your list include some of the following qualities?

- kind
- courteous
- honest

- ethical
- dependable
- good listener

- empathetic
- respectful
- polished professional

Just like a company creates a brand for its corporate entity, each of us creates our personal brand either consciously or haphazardly. If you are short on any of the qualities listed above, you have some work to do on your brand and your character.

Now that we have finished the inside review of Product YOU, let's examine the outside—your packaging.

APPEARANCE AND ATTIRE

Companies spend millions of dollars on the design and packaging of their products because appearance helps to establish brand recognition and consumer loyalty. It also helps attract their desired clientele. With a branding mind-set, let's examine the packaging of Product YOU. Pay attention to your packaging, and you will be able to sell your product more easily. Your overall image is, of course, more than the clothes on your back and the shoes on your feet, but those trappings are what people see first. Your first impression can have a profound impact, because your appearance and attitude are critical factors in how you are perceived initially by others.

FIRST IMPRESSIONS

Business and psychology training literature tell us that there is a five- to ten-second time frame in which to make a first impression. A door in our brain is open for that amount of time when meeting a new person or having a new experience, and then it snaps shut. Blame it on evolution. Primitive man had to make split-second survival decisions (Friend or foe? Flee or fight?), and our brains are wired this way still. If we make a poor first impression, we must work hours, days, weeks, or months to overcome the damage. Why not learn how to make a positive first impression and use it to your advantage? It's like a walk to first base.

Now for the mechanics:

- People form an impression in the first five to ten seconds of meeting someone.
- Fifty-five percent of a first impression is based on appearance.
- Thirty-eight percent of a first impression is based on *how* we speak—our grammar, tone, confidence, and body language.

What does that say about human beings? It says that VISUAL clues and cues shape our initial judgment of people and situations. (Friend or foe? Flee or fight?) Our mothers always told us not to judge a book by its cover—in other words, get to know someone before making judgments about them. Thanks, Mom. Your heart is in the right place, but that's not how our brains work. Until we produce a genetically modified species with a "wait-and-see" chromosome, we will continue to make snap judgments based on first impressions. That's how we are wired.

CLOTHES ENCOUNTERS

You don't have to spend the better part of your salary on clothes in order to be dressed appropriately for an occasion. You need only to be savvy and observant to dress in good taste for *all* occasions. Learn something about the dress code of the environment or industry you're going into, look for clues from others, and ask questions when in doubt.

What's most important to you when selecting clothes for your professional wardrobe? Trends? Color? Fabric? Design? Cost? Correct answer: none of the above. When building your personal brand, your top priority should be *fit*. Do your clothes fit? Money spent on clothing alterations is a good investment. Your neighborhood cleaners can provide alterations or find an independent seamstress or tailor to help you.

Next priority: are your clothes clean and wrinkle-free? Trends, colors, design, and fabric are the frosting, not the cake. Attention fashion renegades: This focus on fit and hygiene is not an attempt to stifle your creativity or squeeze you into a mold. It's a heads-up to underscore that you lose the impact that you're going for if your clothes don't fit or aren't clean.

OLD SCHOOL *VS.* NEW SCHOOL
Dress to Impress

Some things never go out of date. Dressing up to demonstrate respect is one of them. Recently, a young man observed the impact of attire when as an undergraduate premed student he accompanied his father, a doctor, to a medical conference. For travel, the son wore a blazer with an open-neck, collared shirt and dress pants. The father wore a golf shirt, chinos, and a windbreaker. As they stood together at the conference welcome reception, everyone who approached the father-son duo extended a hand and introduced themself first to the son. The father, a world-renowned heart specialist, was the conference keynote speaker the next day, but the twenty-year-old son made a better first impression.

FITNESS REPORT

Are you guilty of any of these fit offenses?

- shirt or jacket sleeve seams droop over shoulders
- sleeves hide your hands or show too much of your wrist

- pants are so long they catch on your heels or drag on the ground, or pants are so short your socks are on display
- buttons strain
- you have a baggy-is-better mentality

DRESS CODE DECODED

Your personal life and your career will take you into many different environments. When you are required to move into unfamiliar territory, one way to fit in more quickly and project the image that you intend to is by choosing appropriate attire. Dress codes vary among generations, industries, cultures, job sites, geographic regions, and occasions, and a one-look-fits-all philosophy is a formula for failure. When preparing for any new occasion—social gathering, job interview, meeting, or business-related special event—do some research to learn about the target environment, industry, occasion, venue, and participants before going to your closet or the mall. When in doubt

- call the host or coordinator to inquire;
- call another guest invited to the same event; or
- dress one level *above* what you think will be appropriate. It is always better to be slightly overdressed than underdressed.

GAUGE IN BRAIN (FORMAL vs. INFORMAL)

You might be surprised to learn that there is a gauge in your brain with one purpose and two settings. The settings on the gauge are *formal* and *informal*, and its sole purpose is to serve as a firm hand to steer you in one direction or the other when you have choices in attire, forms of address, greetings, introductions, communication, and social and business decorum. The default setting on the gauge is *formal*, because we always begin with formality. Why? Because it is difficult to offend someone by being too formal and very easy to give offense when being too informal too soon. By beginning with the needle set on *formal*, we demonstrate respect. Then, as we pick up signals from the people, occasion, and environment around us, we may decide to move the needle toward *informal*. Knowing if and when to move the needle will be a critical component of your success.

CHECKLIST: How Clothes Should Fit

WOMEN

* **Dress** When standing, hem hangs straight and level all around. Neckline, shoulder seams, armholes, and chest lie comfortably flat—no gaping or constricting.

  * **Jacket or Blazer** Shoulders sit flat across shoulder blades without tugging or bulging. Shoulder seam rests on the outer edges of the shoulder bones, not below. Sleeves cover wrist bones when arms are at sides. No pulling or puckering across the chest when buttoned. Ample room to move arms without sleeves feeling tight.

* **Pants** Rise hits at the top of the thigh, close to but not touching the body. When standing, side seams hang perpendicular to the floor and hemline touches the instep and covers half the heel of the shoe. When sitting, a thumb should fit comfortably under waistband.

* **Skirt** When standing, an inch of material should be able to be pinched at the hip, hemline hangs level without rising in the back, slits are closed, and side seams are unpuckered and perpendicular to the floor. Hemline should rise no more than a few inches above the knee when seated.

* **Shirt or Blouse** Front opening does not pull or gap. Arms should be able to move without pulling or constricting. Shoulder seam is centered on the natural shoulder line. When collar is buttoned, ample room to slip two fingers between the neck and the collar. When tucked in, sufficient fabric to raise arms above head without shirt pulling out of the waistband.

MEN

* **Shirt** Hugs the torso without clinging or constricting. Sleeves hug the arms but don't billow. Shoulder seams rest at the outer edge of the shoulder bone, not below. Cuffs fit snugly around the wrists and, with arms at sides, stop where the hand meets the wrist. Collar fits snugly around the neck and, when buttoned, leaves room for two fingers to fit inside comfortably. Shirt remains tucked in when bending over or raising arms.

* **Jacket** Hangs straight down from the armpits; doesn't flare out at the bottom. Shoulder seams rest at the outer edges of the shoulder bones, not below. When buttoned, doesn't pull across the chest.

Sleeve covers wrist bones when arms are at sides. A small amount of shirt collar should be visible above the jacket collar. Length is right if jacket covers the fanny.

* **Pants** Should not fit tightly around the leg nor billow. Single bend in the fabric (called the *break*) where the pant leg hits the top of the shoe (dress pants have a slightly smaller bend than casual pants). No front pleats.

* **Tie** Fits snugly around the neck under the shirt collar without constricting the collar. Length is right if the end of the tie touches the center of the belt when standing. Wide collar gets a large knot. Narrow collar uses a smaller knot.

CHECKLIST: Attire Defined

The following are terms of suggested attire that are often shared verbally or are printed on invitations and event schedules:

* **White Tie** Worn on the most formal occasions. Men: black tailcoat, starched white shirt, waistcoat (vest), white bow tie, black trousers with satin stripe, black patent shoes. Women: floor-length gowns.

* **Black Tie** Women: short or long evening dresses or very dressy separates. Men: black dinner jacket and matching black pants (or white dinner jacket and black pants, in some environments), black patent shoes. Only after 6:00 p.m. Black tie for an afternoon wedding? Not unless you're an attendant!

* **Formal** See "Black Tie" left.

* **Black Tie Optional** This is a disaster waiting to happen. Men who wear a tuxedo can feel overdressed, and those who don't can feel like a party crasher. When deciding what to wear, use your best judgment based on the guest list, what colleagues and friends plan to wear, or call the host to discuss. (If you are the host, don't put your guests in limbo. Decide what look you are going for and tell them.)

* **Festive/Creative Formal** A license to have fun with your formal look. String tie and cowboy boots with a tux, sparkles, exotic accessories or a boa with a gown or little black dress. Why not?!

* **Informal** CAUTION! The traditional interpretation of "informal" was one step below black tie, in other words, cocktail dressy. Women wore very fancy cocktail dresses or dressy dinner suits. Men wore tuxedos or dark suits and ties, never sport coats or blazers. Today the term is misleading and confusing because of its many interpretations. **Semi-formal** is a more modern name for this category and may help guests to better prepare.

* **Business Attire** Men: business suit and tie. Women: dress, suit, or pantsuit. Consider the dress code of the industry hosting the event to determine level of formality.

* **Business Casual** Many industries have an extremely relaxed dress code, and casual or business casual to one firm or industry may not mean the same to another. Always check with your host, and when in doubt, dress one level *above* what you think will be appropriate in order to look professional.

* **Dressy Casual/Smart Casual** Follow guidelines in "Business Casual" or the following: Women: skirt and jacket, tailored dress, or pantsuit. Men: sport coat or blazer with collared shirt (polo or dress shirt), no tie. No jeans.

* **Resort Casual** Attire suitable for patio, poolside, or beach-themed parties such as luaus. When in a business context, clothes are dressier than typical backyard patio attire.

* **Casual** Every event host has a vision for the gathering and a projected attire in mind. When in doubt, ask. Casual is a minefield; proceed with caution.

* **No Mention of Attire** If an event is held immediately after standard business hours, business attire is appropriate. Look for clues in the text of the invitation that will help you to decide what is appropriate (occasion, venue, time of day).

HYGIENE AND GROOMING GUIDE

Now that you're dressed for success, grade yourself on grooming by seeing if your habits fall more often into the yes or no list. Nothing cancels out a great look quicker than dirty fingernails or bad breath.

YES

- **Clothes** Clean and fresh. No spots on jackets, shirts, or ties. No dandruff on shoulders. Odor-free. Wash or send clothes to the cleaners often. And points off for wrinkles.

- **Shoes** Clean and polished. Odor-free.

- **Teeth** Clean and white. Recheck after snacks and meals. Toothpicks are private, not public, as is flossing.

- **Breath** Fresh. Use breath mints often. Severe halitosis may indicate dental or other health problems.

- **Hands** Clean. Wash hands for at least twenty seconds and use hand sanitizer often. Sweaty palms? Antiperspirant on hands may help. Avoid applying lotion prior to meet-and-greet situations.

- **Hair** Clean and shiny. Off your face. Cut or arranged.

- **Fingernails** Clean and clipped or manicured.

- **Glasses** Lenses free from grime. Frames sit squarely on your face.

NO

- **Spreading Germs** Don't cough or sneeze without covering your mouth or turning into the bend of your elbow. Don't use cloth handkerchiefs. Wash hands and use sanitizer often.

- **Body Odor** Bathe daily.

- **Too Much Scent** Don't overdo perfume or body spray. Want to smell good without having family, friends, and colleagues running to open a window? In place of strong perfumes or body sprays, use scented toiletries, hair products, and laundry detergents.

- **Smoker's Breath** Avoid it by brushing teeth often and using breath mints.

And remember that none of this maintenance is conducted in public or in the presence of others.

POSTURE

Are we losing the ability to stand up straight? We're getting close. The cause? The technology slouch. How many hours a day are you curved over a cell phone, laptop, or tablet? If, like most of us, it's more than you like to admit, it may be affecting your posture. Ask a relative or friend to take a candid photo of you, and check your posture. A slouch can suggest that you don't care, are not engaged in the moment, or are sloppy in general. You don't have to walk or sit like a military cadet, but you do want to look like you're confident, hale and hearty, so stand and sit up straight.

GRAMMAR

These are not the best of times for our friend grammar. It's not completely dead, but it's on life support. The brevity in Tweets and text messages ~~have~~ has taken us ~~farther~~ further from full sentences and correct punctuation than ever before There are apps and websites that can conduct a grammar check of your writing and make you look good. Invest the time to find and use them, or pick up a grammar guide at the library or bookstore. ~~Its~~ It's worth your time, because ~~you're~~ your grammar is part of your brand. Write like a professional to be perceived as one. (See chapter 6 for grammar tips.)

SWEARING AND OFFENSIVE LANGUAGE

Nothing tarnishes your brand faster than a four-letter word. You don't have to speak and write like a candidate for sainthood, but you do have to develop etiquette intelligence that helps you know when coarse language or an off-color story is inappropriate. Business settings are definitely not the time to go for maximum shock effect. It's not uncommon for bosses to rank swearing as their number-one etiquette offense committed by employees. Read your audience and context to know when and what you can get away with.

When did profanity become so commonplace? It must have been a gradual change, but now it has reached epidemic proportions. Often, these words are adopted to create a desired image, to give temporary power to those who feel powerless, or for their shock effect. They are becoming routine vocabulary in popular culture.

Every day, we hear things that make us blush, and not when eavesdropping or overhearing quiet, personal conversations that we are not meant to hear. We're hearing obscene words in the context of:

- cell phone conversations in public spaces
- conversations on subway trains or airplanes
- business meetings in person or on the telephone
- or used in anger, fun, or for emphasis or shock value

We can lose the respect of others when we choose to use profanity. Many of the points we might have earned with our skills, experience, appearance, and hard work go out the window when we open our mouth and obscenities spill out.

TIME SENSITIVITY

What do a star athlete, standup comedian, and effective business professional have in common? Wait for it. . . . Timing. Successful people have an acute sense of time. They are attuned to their surroundings, companions, and agenda, and can analyze data they collect to determine the best time to act or when to be still or silent. When you develop timing, you won't blow that opportunity to ask for a favor, a date, a job, a raise, or to make that great first impression because you acted at the wrong time. Only by focusing outward can you develop the skill to read signals from others and interpret the atmosphere around you.

Consistent punctuality says you are organized, have good judgment, can plan ahead, and that you care about others. When you are habitually late, you telegraph the message that your time is more important than the time of others. There will always be circumstances that cause us to be late, but the other 99 percent of the time, it is our responsibility to be on time, especially when it impacts the schedule or stress level of others.

Repeat after me: "If I'm not five minutes early, I'm late." Make this your motto.

FEEDBACK

Manufacturers and service providers constantly ask for consumer feedback in order to tweak and improve their products and services. You should do the same thing. Ask family members, friends, and colleagues for feedback. This is the only way that you will know if how you see your image, attitude, and abilities is how others perceive them. Use feedback to help improve Product YOU.

Here are some tips for receiving feedback:

- Don't be offended or defensive when you receive honest feedback.
- Your goal should be personal growth. Understand that feedback will help you to grow.
- Act on what you hear; change what needs to be changed.
- There is room for improvement in everyone.
- If you seek feedback merely to validate your own ideas or performance, you are entering into the process for the wrong reason.

MY SPACE

The environment that you create for yourself speaks volumes about you. Look around and see what you have built. Organized living and work spaces, or chaos and confusion? Studies have shown that our attitude and performance improve when our environment is clean, organized, and personalized. Your spaces are part of your brand. Do yours enhance your brand or diminish it? Maybe it's time for a my-space makeover. And your vehicle deserves your attention, too. Is it in shape to drive your supervisor to your next off-site business meeting?

WRAP UP

One person can change the world, and you can be that person. With simple gestures like smiling and shaking hands; listening with undivided attention; holding a door for a stranger; allowing a driver to merge in front of you; being a kind relative, friend, neighbor, and colleague; and treating everyone with respect, you can and do change the world.

CHAPTER 2

PEOPLE SKILLS

Have you noticed that some people are naturally comfortable and confident when interacting with others and some seem to struggle with relationships? For those who struggle without the ability to easily connect with others, the path to achieving personal and professional goals is a steeper climb. What's lacking in many cases are people skills.

Defined by the ability to communicate and interact with others in productive ways, people skills account for 85 percent of our success in our personal lives and in our careers. For those of us not born with these skills, there's good news—they can be acquired just as any other life skill. It's worth the time to analyze your skills to see if they are adding to or subtracting from your success.

What's the path to likeability? Either you can download an app that analyzes your text messages to determine if people like you, or you can work to acquire practical skills that will ensure that they do.

TAKE A HARD LOOK AT YOUR SOFT SKILLS

Bravo if the Golden Rule to treat others as you would like to be treated has been a guiding force in your life, but I encourage you to upgrade that rule to platinum status. Coined by motivational speaker Dr. Tony Alessandra, the Platinum Rule encourages you to "treat others the way they want to be treated." It shifts the focus from you and how *you* would like to be treated, to others and how *they* would like to be treated. It requires more effort on your part, as now you will have to determine what makes people tick. What motivates them? What makes them want to work, date, spend time with, or avoid you? What are people skills? We hear this term often but rarely encounter its definition. Simply put, they are the abilities to understand, communicate, and get along with others. This chapter addresses those three simple goals and what it takes to achieve them: meeting and greeting, listening, building relationships, and demonstrating respect.

CHECKLIST: People Skills Twelve-Step Method

1. **Treat others as *they* would like to be treated.** Take time to discover what makes others feel happy, comfortable, and respected.

2. **Focus outward, empathize, help others, and make them feel important.** This requires you to put your personal agenda on the back burner and your phone in your pocket.

3. **Meet and greet people enthusiastically.** Smile, make eye contact, shake hands, and say your name—those comprise the supreme quadrumvirate of people skills. Not only are these skills the launchpad for new relationships, but they are also critical components of maintaining existing relationships.

4. **Be positive.** Always look for the good in people and situations, and project your bright side. Negativity repels people. If it is part of you, you have some work to do.

5. **Be flexible.** Life throws you curve balls and so do people. How you react will determine the tenor of your life ahead. Rigidity and intolerance result in a bumpy ride.

6. **Develop patience.** Slow down; show you understand that people move at different speeds.

7. **Develop conversational skills.** The secret to good conversation is listening, not lecturing. Listen more than you speak. When it's your turn, be brief and let listeners ask for more.

8. **Be an *active* listener.** Do you know how to listen? It requires more than taking earbuds out of your ears. Learn the steps of being an active listener. (See page 20.)

9. **Use and remember names.** Have a system for remembering names so that you can greet others by name, make introductions.

10. **Stay in touch.** Your friends want to hear from you. So do colleagues and clients. It's how you maintain relationships. Write notes, mail milestone cards, and call, email, or text to say hello.

11. **Resolve conflicts.** Learn to control your emotions, analyze concerns, and problem solve.

12. **Demonstrate respect and tolerance.** Deal with people as individuals before mentally assigning them to a group and making assumptions.

CONNECTING AND BUILDING RAPPORT

Have you ever met someone with whom you are immediately comfortable and feel connected? By magic, you're on the same wavelength, have much in common, and share a chemistry that makes it easy to communicate. This may happen occasionally in your personal life, but rarely will it happen in your professional life. In most instances, it takes time and effort to build productive relationships. By learning to connect with others, we streamline this process.

The easiest way to connect is to treat others the way that they want to be treated. But how do we know how someone else wants to be treated? By paying attention to the signals that people send when they interact with others.

You receive encrypted signals transmitted by others through their attire, facial expressions, body language, handshake, personal space, and conversation. You convert those signals to useful information that helps you determine how to react. Your people skills help you unscramble these signals and filter feedback. Your goal is to get on the same frequency with others in order to connect. Not receiving the signal loud and clear? Improve the skills required to tune in more quickly and appropriately.

When you meet a new person, think of yourself as a detective with acute powers of observation, and gather information about your target individual from what you see and hear. Your goal is to spot clues that will provide insight into a person's attitude, agenda, values, operating style, likes and dislikes, and character. You have had this ability to "read" other people since you were a child. Remember sensing the right time to give your report card to your parents or when to ask for a new bike? Resurrect those powers of observation and timing when dealing with the people in your life today.

When you meet someone for the first time, focus on them and their agenda instead of your own. Look for obvious clues that will reveal information about the person and help you connect:

- Are they formal or informal in manner and conversation?
- Do they tend to frown or smile?
- Do they make eye contact, and are they comfortable with it?
- Is their signature stance an open or closed posture? (Learn about body language later in this chapter on page 23.)
- Is their attire conservative, trendy, informal, polished, or sloppy?
- Are they positive, negative, irritated, distracted, whiny, enthusiastic, hassled?
- Are they late, early, or on time?

Look for clues in a home or work space:

- Do they display family, travel, nature photos? What about vanity pictures with VIPs?
- Do they have a disorganized home, car, desk, or briefcase?
- Are there stacks of unread newspapers or correspondence?
- Do they have sports and fitness equipment?
- Is there an art collection?
- Are there fast-food wrappers in their car, home, or office?

Everything that you observe about a person can carry a clue to how best to approach them and interact. Many of these clues will translate into information about

- the best way to approach him;
- what is important to her;
- how the person operates in business;
- what subjects are of interest to her;
- if the person has time constraints; and
- how the person feels about himself and about his family, job, and life in general.

After you have collected information, review it and look for indicators that will reveal personality, interests, the role that their work plays in their life, their stress level, and what they hold near and dear. In other words, you start to get to know someone by looking at the outline of their life. This information will help you to build a relationship, because you will make strategic decisions regarding when to connect (timing of calls, invitations, meetings), how to connect (through mutual friends in an industry, your neighborhood, a service organization, the gym), why to connect (shared social or business interests), and acceptable topics of conversation (family, sports, birds, but perhaps not politics).

Can you always do this amount of preparation when attempting to get to know someone? No, but the method is the same: focus outward, collect information, identify values, show interest, pay attention, and demonstrate respect. Easy! Now you're connecting.

LISTENING SKILLS

One of the most powerful tools to help you in both your personal and professional life is as obvious as the nose on your face—make that the ears on your head. The tool is active listening. Not only is listening a basic element of effective communication, but it is also a cornerstone of people skills. But now hear this: Effective listening takes work. It is not a passive state of suspension, but rather an active process that involves your mind *and* body. By listening in a manner that indicates your desire to hear and understand, you demonstrate interest in the information being conveyed and respect for a speaker. Here's the bonus card in the game: When you listen to others, they tend to return the favor. When you are perceived as a considerate and thoughtful listener, you will be given an opportunity to get *your* message across when it's your turn to speak.

So, what does it take to be a good listener? To begin, it takes your undivided attention. Studies have shown that on average, we can speak about 100 to 150 words per minute, and we are capable of processing up to 400 words per minute. So where is your mind going with all that extra time? Too often it is formulating your response to the comments being made, allowing your eyes to drift over the speaker's shoulder, mentally checking items off your to-do list, debating if you should answer your cell phone; or strategizing how not to be late to pick up your kids (or was it the dry cleaning?). In other words, your mind is wandering, and when your mind is wandering, you're not listening actively.

Super saleswoman Mary Kay Ash said that part of her phenomenal success with Mary Kay Cosmetics was that, when dealing with people, she always pictured a sign around their neck that read "Make me feel important." That is exactly what we are doing when we are being good listeners.

ACTIVE LISTENING

What does it take to be a good listener? Here are some guidelines to help you improve your skills:

Focus Don't let your mind wander, and don't spend too much time thinking about your response. Listening is not biding time, waiting for someone else to finish speaking so that you can speak; it is an active process of hearing and thinking about what is being said. Minimize the attention you pay to the distractions in your head and the environment. Listen more than you speak.

When listening in meetings, ignore cell phones and other electronic devices and no texting. Demonstrate that you are listening by exhibiting appropriate body language, taking notes (see below), and participating in discussions.

Eye Contact Make and maintain appropriate eye contact. Too little or too much makes others uncomfortable. In a North American context, eye contact should be maintained 60–70 percent of the time you spend in conversation. Before you travel, learn the nuances of eye contact in various cultures, because the formula varies around the globe.

Where should eyes go when eye contact is broken temporarily? They should stay within an imaginary triangle that you picture over your speaking partner's head. The apex of the triangle is positioned at the top of the speaker's head, and the base is a line connecting the shoulders. When listeners keep their eyes within the triangle, speakers know they haven't lost attention.

Respond Nonverbally Demonstrate through your body language that you are paying attention and hearing what is being said. Maintain an open posture while listening by aligning your shoulders with your companion's shoulders. Lean in slightly, nod or shake your head, and respond with appropriate facial expressions. Don't cross your arms over your chest or exhibit other closed postures. Avoid hands on hips or in pockets.

Respond Verbally Repeat words or phrases; restate some of the information you have heard; ask follow-up questions; or make comments using information you have heard. This helps the speaker know not only that are you listening, but also that you are processing what is being said.

Don't interrupt, and don't finish someone else's sentence. Allow a speaker to finish entirely before you begin to ask follow-up questions or add your comments. Ask open-ended questions instead of ones that will elicit a yes or no answer.

Respect Personal Space In North America, a comfortable distance between two speakers is approximately thirty inches, the sum total of the length of the two speakers' forearms. Around the world, this space will increase or decrease based on culture. Become a global citizen and adapt.

Process Information I listened; I heard. Now what? Process information that you receive, both while in conversation and after. Remember to consider the context of a conversation, not just the content, in order to fully understand what was said. In a subsequent meeting with the speaker, refer to your last conversation to indicate that you heard and remember what was said. It mattered to you.

CONVERSATIONAL SKILLS

It's easy to be considered a good conversationalist; just be a good listener and ask questions. And, no, it's not necessary to contribute 50 percent of a conversation to be good company, but an occasional pertinent comment goes a long way.

To participate intelligently in conversations, you need to be informed, and not only in areas of your personal interests and professional focus. You need to know a little bit about a lot of things—Hollywood, healthcare, hockey, and history—and the difference between hummus and Hamas. So, *read* a print or online newspaper or news compilation every day or tune in to radio or television news on your way to the kitchen or work. You may have occasion to drop a tidbit of information from this morning's news into your conversation with a client at lunch. Always be prepared to talk to anyone about anything, or, at least, to be an informed listener.

CHECKLIST: Dealing with Difficult People

Don't allow someone else's rude behavior to rub off on you. You control your actions and reactions, so avoid becoming defensive and returning insults. Instead, state that you want to help the offender but that he or she needs to calm down in order for you to understand the problem. Then use some of the following techniques to help defuse the situation and find a solution:

* Listen carefully to complaints. Use active listening skills (see above) to indicate that you hear what is being said.

* Never say no without first asking for additional information.

* Use some of the same words used in the complaint in your response: (I know that you are "angry," "frustrated," "dissatisfied," by "our last discussion," "accounting mistakes," "impersonal service," "staff disregard for rules," "missed deadlines"). By the tone of your voice, show that you care about the situation.

* Respond to *what* is said, not *how* it is said. Try to filter out tone, volume, attitude, and body language to get to the kernel of a complaint.

* Keep your emotions in check. Do not become defensive or allow yourself to be dragged into the fray. Remember, in most instances, negative remarks or complaints are not directed at you. Apply the **QTIP** Rule: **Q**uit **T**aking **I**t **P**ersonally.

* You may need to ask the individual to "Please calm down so that we can find a solution to this problem." If you are unable to reason with a complainer or you feel threatened, ask for assistance from others.

* If appropriate, apologize (at least for the inconvenience caused).

* Ask the individual what they would like to see happen or how they think the issue can be resolved. You may not be able to provide what they ask for, but you may be able to suggest something comparable.

* Clearly state what you plan to do to assist and give a deadline for when you will respond or follow up.

* Keep promises made.

BODY LANGUAGE

What's your body saying about you? Does it speak loud and clear or scramble your message before it reaches the receiver? Most of us are unaware that our body language conveys a wide range of emotions and messages even before we begin to speak: confidence, insecurity, interest, anger, annoyance, stress, resistance, mistrust, dominance, readiness to negotiate, comfort, or distress, to name only a few. As much as 50–60 percent of our message is delivered through these nonverbal cues.

Because of this, it is critical to think about posture, eye contact, gestures, facial expression, placement of arms and feet, and personal space when we are attempting to deliver our message to others.

BODY LANGUAGE LESSON

Face Smile! It says that you are confident, friendly, approachable, caring, nonthreatening, and ready for conversation. Make eye contact when meeting someone or listening while in conversation.

Posture Stand up straight to demonstrate confidence, interest, and respect. Maintain an open posture (face others directly and align your shoulders with those of your companion). Don't cross your arms over your torso, as that can be interpreted as being defensive, inflexible, and attempting to establish a barrier between yourself and a speaker. Don't know what to do with your hands? Body language experts tell us that a confident posture is standing with fingertips together at waist level. Sit up straight with feet flat on the floor to demonstrate interest and respect. To angle the body away from someone when standing or sitting indicates detachment.

Lost in Translation Certain stances and gestures can sabotage your message:
- holding body too stiffly (nervous, lacking confidence, threatened)
- placing hands on hips (aggression, anger, dominance)
- closed fists or not moving hands at all when speaking (uncomfortable, angry, threatened)
- speaking or listening with hands in pockets (disinterest, distraction, withdrawn)
- crossing legs over knee and swinging foot while seated (boredom, disinterest, lack of respect)

- failing to make and maintain eye contact as appropriate to the culture in context (shyness, disinterest, something to hide)
- using hand gestures that can cause offense or misunderstandings to those of other cultures (OK, #1, V for victory, thumbs-up, pointing with the index finger)
- leaning away when in conversation (distrust, disinterest, distraction, personal space has been compromised)
- shrugging one or both shoulders (disinterest)
- relaxing too much in important settings or occasions (poor judgment, lack of interest or respect)
- touching your face, head, or nose (just gross)
- using your left hand (considered unclean in many cultures)

Always think about what your body language is doing to either reinforce or sabotage your message.

HANDSHAKE AND OTHER GREETINGS

What's in a handshake? Can a gesture that takes so little time make a big impact on how you are perceived by others? It can and does. Your handshake is a symbol of your attitude and self-confidence. Make sure that yours is sending the right message.

A firm handshake demonstrates that you are professional, confident, and energetic and that you are eager to meet new people. A limp or bone-crushing handshake leaves a lasting negative impression.

MASTERING THE ART OF MEET AND GREET

How you greet people reveals a great deal about you—your confidence, your attitude, and your polish. Learn to give a good, firm handshake. Begin with your hand perpendicular to the floor with your thumb pointed to the ceiling, and go into your partner's hand until the webs of your hands touch (the space where the base of the thumb is connected to the hand). Wrap your thumb and fingers all the way around your partner's hand, squeeze assertively—not painfully—and shake three to four times. Shaking is generated from the elbow, not the wrist.

Always stand for a handshake in business. In a North American business environment, the space between partners is approximately 2½ feet (more when meeting Asians, less when meeting Latin Americans or people from the Middle East). Never have your left hand in a trouser pocket when shaking hands, and don't feel obligated to return a double handshake (left hand placed over the two hands shaking) or a pat on the upper right arm. Make no comment about a poor handshake.

Maintain an open posture when shaking hands, smile, make eye contact, and say your first and last name. When meeting someone for the first time, always try to say their name as you shake hands, and use an honorific (Mr., Ms., Mrs., Dr., General) and their last name. These rules apply to both men and women in a North American business setting. When meeting people from other countries, research cultural differences in order not to offend others or embarrass yourself. In some cultures, for example, a hug, kiss, or air kiss may accompany that first handshake, while in other cultures, touching the opposite sex is forbidden. You don't want to be taken off guard.

The following rules apply to men *and* women in a North American context.

HUGS AND KISSES

Whoa! It is not appropriate to hug or kiss someone when meeting them for the first time in a North American business environment. When doing so, you are assuming familiarity too soon. This can make others feel uncomfortable immediately, and you will have to work for a very long time to overcome the negative reaction created by the gesture. On subsequent meetings, it is normally the woman who decides if a handshake turns into a pat on the shoulder, a hug, or a kiss on the cheek.

In many cultures, hugging and/or kissing is a traditional part of greeting others, even new acquaintances. Read about cultural nuances before traveling or meeting international business colleagues.

INTRODUCTIONS PLAYBOOK

Making courteous and appropriate introductions is not rocket science, nor is it the easiest thing you will ever have to do. However, with practice, you will become comfortable with the task and accomplish it with ease and very little stress.

Why bother to learn this skill? Because

- it makes people feel comfortable;
- it facilitates conversation;
- it helps to avoid awkward situations;
- you will show others that you are confident and professional; and
- it gives you an advantage, as most people don't know how to do it.

CHECKLIST: Handshake 101

* Face your partner squarely (open posture) when shaking hands, not with right shoulder leading.

* Make and maintain eye contact during a handshake when appropriate to the setting and culture.

* It is not necessary for a man to wait for a woman to initiate a handshake in a North American context.

* In a business setting, men and women stand for a handshake.

* Give a thumbs-up handshake: extend your open-palm hand perpendicular to the floor with thumb pointed to the ceiling. Wrap your fingers around your partner's entire hand at the top where the thumb meets hand. Shake no more than three to four times from the elbow, not the wrist.

* Don't grasp your partner's hand at first knuckle or second knuckle.

* No squeezing and no "limp fish" handshakes.

* Don't place your left hand on top or to the side of the handshake or grab your partner's upper right arm. If your partner does this, you don't have to reciprocate.

* Don't shake hands across a table or desk, either seated or standing. Move to the side or front of the table. Physical barriers can translate to psychological barriers.

* Don't comment on or call attention to a bad handshake.

* Hold a beverage, briefcase, or handbag in your left hand so that you are ready to shake hands at all times.

* If you have sweaty palms, consider using an antiperspirant on your hand before an important occasion or even on a regular basis.

* Avoid putting lotion on your hands immediately before shaking hands.

INTRODUCING YOURSELF

Always be ready to smile, make eye contact, shake hands, and introduce yourself using your first and last name whenever an opportunity arises. Your self-introduction has two purposes: to tell people who you are, and to demonstrate that you are friendly and confident.

When?

- At social or business gatherings—whenever you can
- The person introducing you does not remember your name
- Joining a group already in conversation and no one introduces you
- You recognize someone and he or she does not recognize you
- Seated next to someone at a conference table or dining table
- Going through a receiving line

How?

- Quickly and enthusiastically
- Say your first and last name. Never use an honorific for yourself (Mr., Mrs., Miss, Ms., Dr.). Correct: "Hello, I'm Jane Foster." Incorrect: "Good morning, I'm Miss Foster."
- With a soundbite of information about yourself to place you in context: "I'm Ken Olson from XYZ Company," or "I work with David Barnes," or "I went to school with your daughter, Jean," or "We met at a membership meeting about six months ago."

INTRODUCING OTHERS

In order to simplify, let's break down the process of making an introduction into three steps. Once you know the steps, you will use them each time you are called upon to introduce two or more people.

Three-Step Method

1. Identify an MIP in the twosome or group you will be introducing. What's an MIP? The more/most important person—the higher-/highest-ranking individual in the group.

2. Focus on the MIP, and say his or her name first as you begin the introduction.

3. Introduce others to the MIP.

That's it. Easy! But how do you identify the MIP?

MIP STATUS

Your MIP menu choices are as follows, based on the context of the introduction:

MIP in Business Introductions (Gender-Neutral)

- higher-/highest-ranking individual when introducing people from the same organization or group
- client, visitor, or guest
- official over nonofficial individual
- older individual, if introducing two people of equal rank

MIP in Social Introductions

- newcomer
- woman
- older individual

Process

Assign MIP status to someone in the group of individuals you plan to introduce. From the three-step method above, you will remember to say the MIP's name first and to introduce others *to* the MIP (you are not introducing the MIP *to* others.)

Business Context

For introductions between individuals within the same organization follow the organization chart, and the higher-ranking individual's name is spoken first:

- *"Mr. Senior, I would like to introduce Mrs. Junior to you*."*
- *"Ms. Office Director, I would like you to meet Mr. Recent Hire, our new accounting assistant."*
- *"Dr. Department Chair, may I introduce Ms. Adjunct Professor?"*

* The words "to you" are not always necessary but are included here to underscore the direction of the introduction; it is going *to* the MIP.

Forms of Address

Be consistent with use of honorifics (Mr., Mrs., Miss, Ms., Dr., General). Everyone gets one or no one does. In less formal introductions without honorifics, use the same form of names for everyone, either first name only or first and last name.

Identifiers

If you can, it is a good idea to add a tidbit of information following each person's name to help launch a conversation:

- *"Mr. CEO, may I introduce Ms. Vice President of Sales. She has just joined us from our Dallas office." (and turning to Ms. VP:) "Mr. CEO started with the company in Dallas years ago."*

In business, the *client or guest* when in your "house" is always the MIP, no matter the rank of each individual within their own organization:

- *"Ms. Client, may I introduce Mr. Boss, the president of our company? Mr. Boss, Ms. Client is the Vice President of Sales for XYZ Computers."*

A nonofficial person is introduced *to* an official person (MIP):

- *"Mr. Mayor, may I introduce Ms. Collins, President of ABC Technology? She just joined the board of directors for our charity."*

- *"Dr. Church Minister, I would like you to meet Mrs. Franklin, a new member of the altar guild."*

If you don't know which person outranks the other, or if you think both parties are of equal importance, you must choose which to honor by mentioning his or her name first. In a business context, you could base your decision on seniority but not on gender.

Don't play introduction ping-pong:

- *"Mr. Logan, I would like you to meet Ms. Jenkins. Ms. Jenkins, this is Mr. Logan."*

Instead, say,

- *"Mr. Logan (or David Logan), I'd like you to meet Mrs. Jenkins (or Mary Jenkins.) She is the new human resources associate." (Turning to Mary) "Mary, David will be your point of contact on the Foster project."*

Never skip an introduction you're afraid you won't do it correctly because you don't know the names or you have forgotten someone's name. Attempt the introduction and hope that someone will help you. You'll earn points for trying.

Don't use unnecessary hand or arm gestures. Pointing in any fashion is rude.

Use an honorific until you are invited to use a person's first name.

Just as you would never use an honorific when introducing yourself, don't use one when introducing your spouse or partner. Say, instead,

- *"This is George, my husband,"* or if your spouse's last name is different from your own, *"This is George Ross, my husband."*

NAME GAME
• • • • • • • • • • • • • •

What's an easy way to get someone's attention? Say their name. What's an easy way to make a person feel important and respected? Remember their name the next time you meet. Using and remembering names is a critical soft skill because it's one of the quickest ways to connect with others. It may help you to know that remembering names is a challenge for many people! Showing interest in someone is what matters, and if that means asking them to repeat their name, they won't be offended.

Shakespeare wrote, "What's in a name?" Clearly, a great deal when it comes to building relationships in your personal and professional life. For a large percentage of the population, remembering names is a challenge and something that doesn't come naturally. It takes hard work, but it is a skill that can be developed. And it's well worth the effort. Below are a few tips that can help you win the name game:

Focus Tune out all distractions when meeting others, and focus on faces and names.

Peers vs. Superiors When you meet peers, pay attention to the first name only as you are introduced. If you try to capture all of the information you hear in an introduction—first name, last name, and affiliation—you'll feel overwhelmed. When you are meeting an individual who is senior to you and you want to demonstrate respect, focus on the last name only and use it with an honorific (Ms., Mr., Dr., General):

- *"Dr. Taylor, it is an honor to meet you."*

What's His Name? There is nothing wrong with asking someone to repeat her name; it indicates that you are interested enough to want to remember it. International names are often a challenge, so don't hesitate to ask someone to repeat her name if it is difficult to pronounce.

When meeting a number of people at once, it can be difficult to capture each name. Try to use each name as you shake hands, but it may be necessary to ask the introducer or the person himself to repeat the name. Do the best you can with these multiple introductions, and realize that you may not need to remember each and every name in every group. If they are new coworkers, it will take time to remember all their names.

When you are introduced to someone, try to associate some image or theme with the person and her name. If you have known a Jane before, quickly link the former Jane with the new one in your mind. Or does the person remind you of a celebrity or a character in a novel, TV show, or cartoon with a similar name, face, height, coloring, or interest? If the new acquaintance is David <u>Black</u> and he is wearing black or has black hair, use that as a tag. Or Ann <u>Turner</u>, you talked about a new book . . . page turner. <u>Joseph Woods</u>, maybe he has a wooden countenance with no smile or a moustache like Joseph Stalin? Perhaps Helen <u>Daniels</u> was drinking bourbon. Devise your own system.

When you say goodbye, you might have to ask someone to repeat their name, and at that point, you may be able to associate something you just talked about with their name. The more you practice these name-word associations, the quicker these matchups will pop into your mind as you meet new people. As an exercise, look at the name badges of sales staff the next time you are in a store, restaurant, bank or hotel. Practice linking their names to something that you notice about them. Later in the day, review these people and their names.

Rule of Three Make it a habit to use the name of the individual you are meeting at least three times during your first encounter:

1. When you shake hands or in your first sentence of conversation.
   "Hi, Jane." or *"It's a pleasure to meet you, Peter."*

2. Say the name again during your conversation.

3. Say the name again as you say goodbye. If you didn't retain the name from the introduction, you may say as you are parting:
   "It was great talking with you about the reorganization. Thanks so much for the tip/information/sharing your thoughts. And, please, tell me your name once more. I am sorry; it's been one of those days."

If you don't want to admit at this point that you have forgotten a name, you may offer your social or business card as you part. This might prompt the other person to offer hers. Or you could say,

   "May I contact you for additional information about (the topic you were just discussing)?"

This, too, could prompt the person to offer their card or to jot down their name and number for you.

After you leave a meeting, seminar, or network gathering, write notes about the people you met. Keep the notes chronologically in one place where they will be easy to find for later reference (not scattered around on sticky notes or scraps of paper). If you collect business cards, you may write notes on those ("Met David on 1/27/16 at the XYZ reception/gray suit/bow tie/spoke about California"). Review these notes a day or two later so that the names will stick in your mind. Also, this review will be a reminder to follow up with some or send promised information to others.

FORGOT A NAME? CONFESS OR FINESSE?

What's the best approach when you spot someone you know you've met before but can't remember the name? Confess or finesse it?

It's wiser to finesse for as long as possible:

- *"Hello, I'm Jane Grant. It's so good to see you again! We met at the XYZ reception. Weren't you just starting a new job then?"*

or

". . . about to travel to Spain?"

or

". . . planning your wedding?"

Say this with an enormous smile on your face so that the person can see how delighted you are to see them again. And you dispense even more good will because you remember your previous conversation. After a few minutes, you may pick up the forgotten name indirectly in the conversation or when someone joins your group. If that doesn't happen and the conversation is coming to a close, it's time to confess.

- *"It was nice to see you again. And, please remind me of your name."*
- *"David Hynes."*
- *"Oh, yes, of course!"*

By then you've already reconnected, so admitting you forgot the name isn't such a blow.

When you are called upon to introduce others and have forgotten names, you can say to both:

- *"Have you met?"*

There will be a short pause, they will introduce themselves to each other, and you can capture their names as they do so. You get credit for setting up the introduction but don't have to say the two names.

Another method to orchestrate introductions in groups is to say,

"Why don't we all introduce ourselves."

Begin by introducing yourself.

NETWORKING ETIQUETTE

Networking experts and literature tell us that networking is a necessary evil of expanding our horizons and, more specifically, our contacts. We are told we "need to get out there" and promote ourselves and our professional agenda. But why look at it as a painful procedure? It is simply communicating with others at any time or place, so you're already engaged in this practice every day of your life. Networking is not always looking for a job lead or attempting to make a sale. It is happening any time people come together to small talk, get to know one another, share ideas, vent, commiserate, or just hang out. If you want to become more comfortable and proficient when networking is structured into a professional gathering, adopt some of the following strategies, suggested by the experts, the next time you attend an event or gathering.

BEFORE YOU GO

- When you receive an invitation to a networking event, *respond!* It's rude not to do so.

- Have a reason to attend an event. If you attend because you are a member of the host organization, want to hear a speaker, support a cause, are seeking more information about an industry, or have an interest in the venue, you'll be more comfortable and engaged.

- Do your homework. Learn as much as you can about the event, host, speaker or honoree, other attendees, and the occasion.

- Identify your goals for the event (e.g., meet ten new people, learn more about the host organization, talk to someone in your target field, improve your conversational skills). Your primary goal should not be to distribute your business card.

R U RUDE? Transgender Courtesy

Courtesy is contagious. When we demonstrate respect for transgender individuals, we influence others around us to do the same. But how do we know the right thing to do and say to demonstrate respect to the transgender community? We start by understanding the accepted terminology.

The National Center for Transgender Equality tells us that the term **transgender** identifies "people whose gender identity, expression, or behavior is different from those typically associated with their assigned sex at birth." **Gender identity** refers to a person's own sense of being male, female, or something else. And **gender expression** refers to the way a person communicates their gender identity to others through behavior, clothing, hairstyles, voice, or other characteristics.

A quick look at some of the mistakes others make when interacting with transgender individuals will help us to avoid offending or embarrassing transgender family members, friends, or colleagues in our lives.

R U RUDE?	CORRECTIVE MEASURES
You ask a transgender individual, "What's your real name?"	RUDE and insensitive. The individual may have just told you his real name, the name he adopted in his new gender identity. Don't ask personal questions dealing with life before transitioning, family reaction or support, or medical treatments past, present, or future. If a person wants to talk about these things, he will bring them up. If you are in a position where you are required to know the individual's legal/birth name (such as human resources or law enforcement), do your best to respect the individual's preferred name when speaking with him.
You just learned that someone in your office is transitioning. Shouldn't you tell your coworkers so that they can avoid blunders?	RUDE and inappropriate. If a transitioning individual wants to share this personal information with business colleagues, the conversation must be initiated by her, not by you. Just as you wouldn't want your personal information to be shared without your permission, you must respect the individual's privacy.

R U RUDE?	CORRECTIVE MEASURES
You ask a transgender colleague, "So, what are you, gay, lesbian, or bisexual?"	RUDE and misinformed. This is a rude question to ask anyone at any time. But since you asked, gender identity and sexual orientation are not the same. Sexual orientation refers to an individual's sexual attraction to another person, whereas gender identity refers to one's own sense of being male or female. Transgender people can be straight, lesbian, gay, bisexual, pansexual, or asexual, just as cisgender (non-transgender) people can be.
You have known a friend as a man for many years and he—she?—now wears long hair and a dress. How should you react? Do you treat him the way you used to, or forget your former friend because it is too complicated for you?	Not RUDE, just confused. Your friend is still your friend, and you should treat her as you always have, with kindness and respect. And to demonstrate your friendship, you need to applaud her for her courage and accept her new look. Her hair and clothing are part of gender expression, which is how transgender people represent their identity to others—through behavior, clothing, hairstyles, voice, or body characteristics. If you are having trouble adjusting, have a frank and honest talk with your friend, and tell her you are struggling with her new identity. Try to tell her you support her decision and that she will always be your friend.
At a holiday gathering, you ask your transgender cousin, "Are you a he or a she now?"	Not RUDE, just obtuse. It is important to use the pronouns (he/him/his or she/her/hers) that correspond to an individual's gender identity, but you may not have to ask if you pay attention to the individual's name, attire, and other gender expressions. If you do ask, ask privately, and something more along the lines of "Do you go by Mr. or Ms.?" (similar to asking a woman if she prefers Ms. or Mrs.). If you make a mistake in conversation, apologize and try to get it right in the future. If no one notices, don't call attention to it by overcorrecting. When unsure of what's correct, stick to using gender-neutral pronouns and language. And remember to choose the correct honorific when formality requires use of someone's full name in print or conversation: Mr., Ms., Miss, or the new Mx. (pronounced mix).
A family member is crossing over, and you don't know what to say, so you have been avoiding him/her.	RUDE and unkind. Often we avoid difficult conversations because we are afraid of saying the wrong thing, but that is putting your own feelings before those of your relative who needs support at this time. It took courage for the individual to share the news of his or her transitioning (not "crossing over"). Thoughtful and appropriate responses to this news would have been: "I'm glad you told me," "I support your choice," or "Please know that you can talk to me."

- If you suspect that you will be uncomfortable, plan to arrive at the beginning of an event. It is easier to wade into a small group of attendees than to dive into a sea of people.
- Think about what you will say when asked the dreaded question, "What do you do?" Prepare a reply in two parts: a pithy statement describing you, your interests, and your goals; and follow-up information that you will share when someone wants to hear more.

DURING THE EVENT

- Remember that your number-one goal is to connect with people, not to sell.
- Turn off your cell phone. *Off*, not silenced.
- If you attend with a colleague, split up after you check in. You'll meet more people.
- Practice active listening techniques, and make appropriate eye contact.
- Listen more than you speak.
- Ask open-ended questions.
- Wear a name badge if they are provided.
- Use and remember names.
- Don't spend too much time with one individual.

- Food and beverage are not your main focuses.
- Use polite exit strategies to leave a conversation (e.g., refresh your drink, make a call, locate a colleague, consult with an individual from a particular organization, or introduce someone else to the person to whom you are speaking and exit the conversation).
- Distribute business cards *after* connecting with individuals and only if there is a reason to share your contact information.
- Thank the host or host representative before you leave, if possible.

AFTER THE EVENT

- Make notes about contacts you made.
- Review your "networking performance." If given a do over, what would you change? How can you improve?
- Follow up. Connect with new contacts through social media. If you have offered to share something with someone (e.g., a telephone number, a link to a website, an introduction, your contact information) or you have offered to get in touch later, *do so*. One of the most important networking goals is to build your reputation as a responsible and caring individual.

- Send a handwritten thank-you note to your host, if appropriate. This won't be necessary for every event you attend, but it is a way to cement a connection.

DISABILITY ETIQUETTE

Often, we are awkward when meeting and interacting with people with disabilities because of *our* shortcomings, not theirs—we think *we* will do or say the wrong thing. The guidelines below—developed by professionals who provide services to this community, with input from their constituents—will help you get it right.

PEOPLE-FIRST LANGUAGE

The best place to start is to adopt a vocabulary that demonstrates respect. Members of the community ask us to focus on *people* first and disabilities second, so appropriate language is called people-first language. The individual should precede the mention of his or her disability when speaking or writing about members of the community. It underscores that individuals are not defined by their disability: John is in a wheelchair, Margaret is visually impaired, Adam walks with crutches, a person with cerebral palsy, a woman who is visually impaired, a teen who is deaf—all are *people* with disabilities.

Relax, the rest of your vocabulary doesn't need an overhaul. It is OK to use phrases and idioms that include references to sight, sound, or mobility, such as "See what I mean?" or "I know you have to be running along." Don't try to overcorrect when you use these words, because then things *will* get awkward.

GENERAL GUIDELINES

YES

- Be courteous, not condescending or overprotective. A pat on the head, arm, or shoulder is offensive.
- Speak with adults with disabilities like adults.
- Direct your attention and comments to the individual with the disability, not to a guide, aide, companion, or sign language interpreter.
- Use a normal tone of voice. Don't speak louder to a person with a disability. It demonstrates a lack of knowledge and sensitivity.

- Offer help in general terms as you greet or escort someone with a disability: "Please let me know if I may help in any way. I'll be with you throughout the morning." Never act before your offer is accepted, and, if it is, ask for instructions on how to proceed: "Would you like to take my arm?" or "How can I help?" Don't enlist the help of others without a specific request to do so.

- Offer your hand for a handshake if you are not familiar with the individual's ability to shake hands. If you have to make a correction, do so with a smile. It is OK to shake hands with your left hand if the person whom you are meeting offers their left hand. If a person cannot shake hands, your smile and words of welcome are sufficient greeting.

NO

- Avoid the following terms: handicapped, disabled, confined to a wheelchair, wheelchair-bound, victim, afflicted, or suffers from . . .

- Don't stereotype. Treat people as individuals with specific capabilities.

- Don't ask personal questions about a person's disability.

- Do not touch mobility devices; they are extensions of an individual's personal space. Don't lean on a wheelchair or scooter or hand a cane or crutches to an individual without their requesting it.

- Do not touch or pet a service animal.

SPECIFICS

People Who Use a Wheelchair

- Don't touch a wheelchair. Don't attempt to move the chair without a request to do so.

- Point out obstacles when moving through a building or terrain that is familiar to you but is unfamiliar to your companion.

- Sit to talk to an individual in a wheelchair if you will be speaking for longer than a quick greeting. Find a chair and sit to be at eye level; don't squat or kneel next to a wheelchair with your hand on the chair arm or back.

Blind or Vision Impaired

- Speak to the individual as he or she enters a room to inform him or her of your presence.

- Introduce yourself and others who are with you.

- If you are accompanying a person with a visual impairment, offer your forearm or elbow and mention obstacles as you approach. "I'll be going with you to the conference room. Would you like to take my arm?" Narrate while you walk, and inform the individual when you have arrived at your destination. "We'll be going thirty feet ahead to the end of the corridor where we'll be turning right into the conference room."

- Say goodbye when you leave a room or conversation.

Deaf or Hearing Impaired

- Do not raise your voice or shout when speaking.

- Wave or tap a person on the shoulder or forearm to get their attention.

- Not all individuals with a hearing impairment are lip readers. If they are, face the individual directly, speak slowly, and keep hands and other objects away from your mouth.

- It is not necessary to include a sign language interpreter in your conversation, but politely acknowledge them when they join or leave the group.

Speech Impaired

- Be patient and understanding. Don't try to rush a conversation.

- Make and maintain eye contact when listening. Don't focus on the speaker's mouth.

- Use a normal tone of voice.

- It is not helpful, but rather it is insulting to try to help someone find a word or finish a sentence.

- If you did not hear or understand what was said, paraphrase what you think was said or ask the individual to repeat it.

CHAPTER 3

YOUR WORLD

There are so many opportunities each day for us to be courteous and kind. Look around your world to see where you can help your neighbor. Promoting civility can help to build communities by recognizing the rights of all, using peaceful discourse when conflicts arise, and respecting all opinions and voices.

LIVING WITH MANNERS

Some elements of neighbor relations have not changed in centuries. We continue to wage war or build mutually beneficial relationships based on differences or similarities in values, interests, personal space, behavior, money, possessions, animals, and the company we keep. Whether you live in a crowded apartment building or on a ten-acre property, you have neighbors and must attempt to coexist peacefully. Good neighbor relations, like all relationships, take work. There is give-and-take, highs and lows, and you can't always have it your way. One way to minimize wars and maximize benefits is to install civility in the core of your good-neighbor policy. Simply put, be polite, reasonable, and respectful.

MOVE-IN-READY MANNERS

When you move into a new home—dorm room, apartment, condo, co-op townhouse, house, trailer, or tent—you're joining a community, and communities have rules, both written and unwritten. Your responsibilities to the community begin on day one, so be sure to unpack them first.

Learn as much as you can about the governance of your new community before moving in. Is it rigid or flexible? Quick to solve problems or slow as molasses? Democratic or dictatorial? Ask current residents for input, if possible.

Ask about community restrictions covering move-ins. Does your landlord, homeowners' association, resident advisory board, or local government have quiet hours or other rules that will affect your plans? In apartment buildings, check with management for time frames for using elevators and moving equipment. Don't capture elevators for long periods of time without permission. Don't block sidewalks, driveways, or hallways with handcarts, cars, or moving trucks.

Smile and introduce yourself to neighbors in hallways, on elevators, or in the street. Apologize for disruptions caused by your move.

WELCOME WAGON

New neighbors just moved in? It's time to welcome them to the floor, building, block, or community. If you have their telephone number, call ahead to ask for a convenient time to "drop by" (don't say "visit," because then your coming turns into a big deal for them). If it's not possible to call ahead, ring their doorbell, stay at the door or on the porch, and deliver your quick welcome greeting. Don't expect to be invited in. *Do not* bombard new neighbors with personal questions or go inside for a long conversation. You can make a date for that later (the conversation, not bombardment).

Bring a welcome note and something practical—cookies (always useful); fresh fruit, vegetables, or other local specialties; a snow shovel if they just moved from Florida to the snow belt. Ask if there is something they need—cleaning supplies, trash bags, a box cutter, a list of local resources?

APARTMENT, CONDO, CO-OP, AND TOWNHOUSE LIVING

It's difficult today to know how to be a good neighbor, especially when we are sharing a building with others. Communal living brings out the best and worst in all of us. The headaches that can develop when we share floors, ceilings, walls, and sometimes rooms call for extra-strength courtesy.

ROOMMATE RULES

Discuss and establish ground rules on day one of living together, or, better yet, before moving in together. What will be permitted and what won't be tolerated regarding expenses, furniture and equipment, cleaning, shopping, cooking, thermostat settings, visitors, noise, borrowing stuff, privacy, and time spent together? You may not need to draft and sign a ten-page roommate agreement, but you do need to have a discussion.

Not all roommates are best friends, nor is it necessary that they become so. Don't assume that you need to do everything together. Respect private time and time spent with other friends that doesn't include you.

Create and post a communal list of contact information: phone numbers, email addresses, and emergency contacts. Create and enforce a key policy. How many keys are there? Who has them? Who can say yes or no on making copies? If keys are lost, who pays to have the locks changed?

And respect the unwritten code of honor: roommate information is private. Don't share it with others.

Dorm Rooms

Everyone knows that the first room-mate to arrive on move-in day gets to choose the best space, right? But maybe, to make things fair, you could go with a coin toss to decide who chooses first, and start off on the right foot. It's also a good idea to find out if a roommate has special needs that might preclude your choice.

Apartments, Condos, Co-ops, and Townhouses

If you are joining an established group of housemates, refer to the roommate agreement discussion topics above. It is especially important that you know and follow the house rules, because you are entering a pre-existing domestic ecosystem, and your goal should be not to upset it. You do not want to hear the dreaded words "That's not how we do things here." So, respect the rules, blend in, observe, and pay your dues (as well as your rent) before suggesting changes to the system.

When individual spaces within a unit are not equal in size, there should be adjustments in rent to address it. Determine if a seniority system will be in play for claiming larger spaces as they become available when a roommate leaves.

CHECKLIST: Communal Living

Below is a courtesy checklist for apartment, condo, co-op, and townhouse dwellers. When we pay attention to our behavior in these areas, there are fewer disputes, frayed nerves, hurt feelings, angry outbursts, or trips to defend ourselves before the resident advisory board.

* **Smile and Acknowledge Neighbors** Greet neighbors in hallways, elevators, lobby and parking areas, and extra points earned for a "good morning" at the Dumpster. Nobody wants to live near a grump.

* **Help Others** Check on elderly residents who live alone, and offer assistance to neighbors who may need help with routine chores. Be mindful of the safety of children who live nearby. It takes a building.

* **Noise** It's the number-one neighbor vs. neighbor complaint. Follow the rules in your resident handbook covering quiet hours, floor coverings, use of appliances, music (live and recorded), parties, and supervising children. If a neighbor has a reasonable complaint, try to abate your noise to accommodate their request.

* **Trash** Your trash is no one's treasure, so keep it contained and out of sight. Check to see if specific garbage, recycling, or composting containers are required. Seal bags securely before placing them into containers. Don't overload trash chutes or Dumpsters.

* **Laundry Rooms** Don't monopolize machines for long periods of time. Because you do laundry once a month . . . on Saturday does not mean that you can use the machines for an entire day. Wait a respectful period of time before removing someone else's clothes from a machine. If you do, place them on top of a machine or folding table, never on the floor. Don't use someone else's laundry supplies.

* **Common Areas** Party rooms, patios, rooftop decks, and communal green spaces are for all residents to share. Don't monopolize them. Be mindful of the noise and trash that you and your guests generate in these areas, and how it affects not only the neighbors in adjacent quarters but the entire complex as well. Remember that you are responsible for your guests' behavior.

* **Pools and Fitness Rooms** Follow guidelines for hours of use, noise and hygiene, and dress discreetly. Supervise children in these areas.

* **Parking** Park in appropriate spaces and within the lines of each space. Give clear parking instructions to your guests. Don't double park, even for short periods of time.

* **Pets** Keep dogs on leash when moving through your building. Clean up after your pets in shared outdoor areas. Barking dogs and howling cats are a nuisance to all. If you have one, be prepared to find solutions that you can share with neighbors when they come knocking on your door to complain.

* **Smoking** Ask about smoking restrictions before moving in. Some buildings are completely smoke-free, as are their grounds. If smoking is permitted in your space, remember that smoke travels through walls and doors, so ventilate. When smoking in shared outdoor areas, position yourself downwind of others when possible, and don't drop cigarette butts on the ground.

SINGLE-FAMILY HOMES

With more space comes more responsibility to be a good neighbor. Each day, think about how your words and actions impact your neighborhood and community.

Neighborhood Nice

When the new-neighbor honeymoon ends, and it will, problems will begin to sprout like dandelions. Address a problem soon after it arises and before your anger and resentment boil over. Speak with a neighbor politely and positively when you go to discuss a problem. Offer solutions, not only complaints. Cookies work here. Approach a neighbor with them in hand, politely mention the problem or concern, remain calm and polite, and suggest a solution. Be diplomatic; don't involve a third party (neighborhood association or local authority) until you have exhausted the neighbor-to-neighbor approach. And don't complain about every trivial thing that annoys you. Neighbors will learn to tune you out.

Noise isn't nice, so keep yours to a minimum. Find out if there is a local noise ordinance that can give you some guidance. Be mindful of outdoor speakers, lawn mowers, leaf blowers, car tune-ups, parties, and construction noise. In most areas, regulations prohibit noise before 9:00 a.m. on a Saturday or Sunday, and they are enforceable.

We know from Benjamin Franklin and his *Poor Richard's Almanac* that it's a bad idea to be a borrower or a lender, so think twice before you do either. But if you do lend your possessions, devise a simple tracking system or create a log into which you can record the item, date, and borrower's information. Record data while borrower is present.

Curb Appeal

The next time you leave home, stop at the curb, turn around, and take an objective (try!) look at the front of your house and yard. What you see in that few seconds is what your neighbors have to look at every day. Orange shutters and chartreuse siding? Not a problem—colors and design are your choice (unless you are ignoring the covenant of a homeowners' association). But uncut grass, mounds of trash, abandoned building supplies, and assorted auto parts? Those are not only eyesores but dangerous as well because they are tripping hazards and can attract rodents and other pests. Violations and fines are a possibility. Your front yard doesn't have to win a garden club award, but it does need to be neat and meet local ordinances. Be a good neighbor. Clean up! PS Now work on your side and back yards. Some of us can see those, too. Thanks!

If you have a neighbor whose yard is in need of a major tune-up, speak with them directly, neighbor to neighbor, before going to a higher authority. Offer a solution, not just a complaint. Remember to bring the cookies. Can't hurt; might help. And offer to pitch in to help when a neighbor needs assistance due to illness or other hardship.

Sidewalks should also be a concern to all home renters and owners. If concrete or stones are cracked or out of alignment, they are tripping hazards and should be repaired. Local ordinances may require the property owner to do so. Always keep walkways cleared of ice or snow as soon after a snowfall as possible. Offer help to neighbors who may not be able to do this themselves.

Trashed

Follow the rules established by your community for trash disposal. Store trash in covered bins prior to pick up so that it won't attract animals or other pests and won't blow around on a windy day. It's nice when it is out of sight from the street, but we don't live in a perfect world, so do your best to camouflage it. Recycle, if you are able to do so, and don't cheat or cut corners in the process. Don't be the neighbor who, preparing to go out of town, puts trash and recycling bins in the street five days before the scheduled pickup. Hey, neighbor, we all have to look at those bins for *five days*. Ask a neighbor to put them out (and bring them in) on the designated day.

Parking

Let's get this question out of the way right away: No, you don't own the on-street parking spaces directly in front of your house unless you live in a community where parking is reserved by name or number. Please, don't complain to neighbors or their visitors who park in "your spot," unless it is a chronic problem that results in your rarely being able to park in front of your house. If so, speak with the offending neighbor politely and try to work out a win-win solution. Cookie diplomacy will help here, too.

Do provide parking guidelines for your visitors so that your neighbors aren't glowering through the mini blinds. These parking concerns become an issue only during extended stays, not during drop-by visits or parties with courteous guests.

When numerous driveways limit available curb parking, park strategically. Don't park in the middle of a curb area that can hold two cars. Don't leave a car parked on the street for weeks at a time without moving it.

Don't park too close to a driveway apron, making it difficult for cars to pull in or out. Leave at least a five-foot space between your car and the apron. The same rule of the driveway applies for curb cuts. When parking multiple cars in your driveway, try not to block the sidewalk.

Snow Business

There's no easier way to alienate a neighbor than by parking in the curbside spot that took him or her hours to shovel out on a snowy morning. Long story short, if you didn't shovel the parking spot, *do not park in it!* Period. When neighbors follow this rule, no one has to look at lawn chairs, orange cones, or other paraphernalia placed in the street to reserve the open spot.

Offer to help with clearing cars of snow, shoveling sidewalks, and taking trash bins to the curb if you have neighbors who need assistance.

Flag Protocol

If you display a US flag on the outside of your house, it should be placed in the position of honor: right side of the front door as you are leaving the house (left side of front door when viewed from the street.) State, city, or other flags are positioned on the other side of the door. When hanging a flag vertically on the outside of a house or building, position it so that the union (stars) are to the viewer's left and the stripes are to the right.

Constructing Relationships

Look around your neighborhood, and you'll probably see at least one construction project underway. Growth and change are inevitable, and so are neighborhood complaints associated with the projects. If you are the root cause of the construction, you have responsibilities beyond planning and funding the project. You have an obligation to your neighbors to keep disruption to a minimum and to see that the project has little to no impact on their property or on communally shared areas.

Don't let your dream project become a nightmare for those around you. When your new addition is standing strong and shiny, will your relationships with your neighbors be in the same shape?

Inform adjacent neighbors about an impending project. Let them know about the plans and schedule and that you will do everything you can to minimize the disruption to your street. Then keep your word. It's not just fences that make good neighbors, it's also informing neighbors when a fence is about to be built.

Give your contractor clear guidelines on parking construction vehicles, delivering and storing materials, Dumpster and Porta-Potty placement, protecting plants and trees, chemical runoff concerns, and your preferred (sometimes mandated) start and end times for work. (If weekend work is planned, it's rude to begin to make noise before 9:00 a.m.) Ensure that all of your guidelines are followed. Your neighbors will let you know if they are not. Give them your contact information so that they can reach you to report concerns.

It's Not Easy Going Green

Recycle in containers provided by your community or local jurisdiction or purchase your own. No bins or containers? Use plastic bags or paper bags according to local guidelines. Do not attempt to recycle toxic substances with regular household recyclables. Check community guidelines for directions.

Read labels and check with your local agricultural extension agency before spreading or spraying chemicals on lawns and gardens. Move bird feeders, birdbaths, and pet food and water dishes away from areas to be treated, and cover fish ponds. Don't pour chemicals down a storm drain or your sink.

Don't water lawns or gardens when restrictions are in place. Place hoses carefully so that water lands on the garden or lawn, not the driveway or sidewalk.

Clear your property of standing water that can breed mosquitoes and attract other pests. Even a bottle cap with water can serve as a breeding ground.

In most jurisdictions, you are permitted to trim tree branches that extend over your property line from an adjacent property, but be courteous and notify your neighbor before doing so. Incorrect pruning can damage a tree.

Pets

Man's best friend can be a neighbor's worst headache. Living with the incessant noise of a barking dog leads to frayed nerves and unraveled neighbor relations. If you live within range of a chronically barking dog, speak politely with the dog's owner before going to a higher authority. Let your neighbor know what you are experiencing and discuss solutions; don't just spit out complaints. No luck with your neighbor? Look into animal-control laws to learn what the next steps might be.

When your dog is outside in your yard, he must be on leash or your yard must be fenced.

Keep your dog on leash when walking through neighborhoods, and don't allow him to urinate on a neighbor's lawn. It kills the grass. Don't let him poop on a neighbor's lawn, shared green space, sidewalk, or in the street, unless you are prepared to pick it up and take it away. If you have a dog walker, tell them that this task is mandatory. Remember that after dark the honor system goes into effect. Just because no one is watching doesn't make it OK for you to break these rules. You know who you are, and with the increase in the number of video home surveillance systems, your neighbor will know who you are, too. Gotcha!

Always ask permission before petting a dog walking with its owner or before offering food or a dog treat. Don't bring a dog, or any pet, to someone's home without checking first with your host.

Cats are another story. Because their trajectory cannot be predicted or controlled, it's useless to complain about their wanderings, howlings, or droppings. If you witness an offense on your property and you can identify the offender, speak politely with your cat-owner neighbor to find a solution. If you catch your feline in the act of leaving a gift on a neighbor's lawn, stoop and scoop. In order to reduce the instances of nighttime howling, cat owners are encouraged by the American Society for the Prevention of Cruelty to Animals (ASPCA) to bring a cat inside at dusk or, even better, to keep them inside at all times.

Thinking about buying or adopting an exotic pet? Check local ordinances before doing so. You may be endangering not only the animal but your family and neighbors as well.

Neighborhood Watch

You are fortunate if you live in an area where neighbors have banded together to create a formal or informal neighborhood watch group to prevent crime or vandalism. Guidelines covering the rights and responsibilities of group members are available from local law enforcement authorities.

Membership in a neighborhood watch program is not license to enter neighbors' yards or peer through windows unless there is imminent danger. Be vigilant but not intrusive. Report suspicious activity to local authorities. Do not attempt to intervene.

When a neighbor leaves their house key with you to be used in case of emergency, it is not an invitation to enter their house for a casual look around.

Adopt the now well-known law enforcement phrase "If you see something, say something" and apply it in your neighborhood.

RETAIL RUDENESS

Each of us experiences retail shopping in a different way. For some it's a necessary evil; for others, a favorite pastime. To prevent it from ever becoming a contact sport, let's look at some of the ways that shoppers and store staff can eliminate rudeness from the roles they play and make shopping a more pleasant experience on both sides of the counter.

ATTENTION, SHOPPERS

When the door swings open for you at the big-box store, upscale boutique, department store, or the local mom and pop, do you leave the cares of the day at the entrance, or do you drag them into the store like an overloaded shopping bag? Do you walk in expecting the best or the worst? It's not rocket science to know that there is a direct correlation between the attitude we bring and the type of shopping experience we will have. Assume you will have a pleasant experience until proven otherwise.

Random Retail Kindness

Treat sales staff with respect and courtesy. They are professionals doing their jobs, which is to help you. Don't direct your anger or frustration toward them when it is a result of the store's faults or shortcomings. Why bite the hand that helps you? Go to a sales manager or to customer service to register a complaint.

Don't monopolize the time of a sales associate if you cannot decide on a purchase. Allow him or her to help someone else while you debate your choices. Don't interrupt sales staff when they are assisting other customers.

When you have been undercharged for items you are purchasing, it is not only rude but also dishonest to fail to tell the sales associate or management about the error. The associate may be held responsible for any discrepancies that occur while they are on duty.

While checking out, don't leave to get forgotten items when others are waiting behind you unless you plan to go to the end of the line when you return. Don't ignore the limit on the number of allowable items in express checkout lines.

When you see someone behind you with two items and you have twenty, allow them to go ahead of you. You won't feel so rushed, and a random act of kindness can have a positive effect on both giver and receiver.

R U RUDE? Manners Markdowns

Below is a dirty dozen of customer rudeness in the context of retail shopping. If you recognize yourself in any of these examples, you may want to think about your shopping habits.

R U RUDE?	CORRECTIVE MEASURES
1. You routinely remove items from sealed packaging to touch, smell, weigh, unfold, feel, or experience a product.	RUDE and affects the stores' bottom line. Opened packages that can't be sold translate to money lost for a store. Ask for assistance if you must have a 3-D product experience before buying. Often, display or tester samples of products are available, or a sales associate will open a package for you.
2. Food shopping for you means squeezing, smelling, handling, and sometimes tasting unwrapped food.	RUDE and unsanitary. Some squeezing of fruit and vegetables is expected, but please don't let that cantaloupe touch your nose. Most grocery stores now have hand sanitizer wipes at every entrance. It's a good idea to wipe your hands and the handle of your cart when you enter, and several times during your shopping trip. You're protecting yourself as well as others. And put down those grapes. They aren't for in-store munching!
3. You fail to place empty carts in roundup areas in the parking lot or garage.	RUDE and lazy. Corral the cart. When you leave them elsewhere, they can roll and injure people or damage vehicles.
4. You attempt to use expired coupons.	RUDE and a little shady. It's not worth having harsh words with a staff member or manager to save a few cents. Unless a store advertises that they recognize a grace period on expired coupons, play by the rules.
5. You fail to monitor children's behavior while shopping.	RUDE and dangerous. Children can cause chaos when unsupervised in a store. Their exuberance can result in injury to themselves or others and damage to store inventory or equipment.
6. You try on clothes without proper undergarments or shoes without a foot covering.	RUDE and gross. Enough said.

7. Using a sales associate's name to get better service always works for you. "David, here's what I need. These green beans look a little tired. I'm sure that you have others in the back."

RUDE and manipulative. Retail employees wear name badges, but that doesn't give you license to overuse their name for your benefit. Unless you know the individual from the community or from having dealt with them in the store on a regular basis, it is rude to use their name to get more attention for yourself. If you have read that this technique will help the employee to bond with you and therefore take more interest in serving you, read instead the Golden Rule, which takes precedence over any other rule or strategy.

8. You talk on your cell phone when a staff member is assisting you with your purchase.

RUDE and rude some more. When the sales associate has to ask you the same question three times, it's time to hang up. There is conversation in a sales transaction, and your attention is necessary to make the process run efficiently. And besides, it's just plain rude to carry on a face-to-face conversation while on your phone. Pay attention to the sales associate and to your transaction.

9. After looking at items on a table or counter or in a fitting room, if they fall to the floor, you leave without picking them up. There are staff members paid to do that.

RUDE and imperious. If you dropped it, pick it up. If you tried it on, return it to a hanger.

10. You have abandoned a cart when you realized it wasn't yours.

RUDE and thoughtless. Not your cart? Take it to customer service and ask for an announcement on the PA system.

11. When deciding not to purchase a refrigerated item you have in your cart, you leave it on an unrefrigerated shelf.

RUDE and wasteful. The item will have to be thrown away when it is discovered by a staff member because of food safety regulations. Don't want to walk all the way back to aisle one to return that yogurt? Take it to customer service, and they will do it for you.

12. You stand too close to others in a checkout line.

RUDE and annoying. Don't crowd the shopper who is paying for purchases, don't send your items careening down the self-check conveyor belt when the shopper in front of you is still loading bags, don't stand near a shopper who is speaking with the pharmacist, and don't crowd others waiting at a service counter that doesn't provide next-in-line numbers.

Help other shoppers who may not be able to reach an item on a high shelf, can't locate an item, or have difficulty navigating a revolving door, carrying boxes or bags, or understanding local currency.

Excuse yourself politely when it is necessary to pass another shopper in a crowded aisle. Omit any attitude of exasperation from the encounter.

When approaching a counter without a system of next-in-line numbers, notice who is waiting before you arrived in order to roughly determine the order of the informal queue. If someone jumps ahead of you, politely say with a smile, "I think I was next in line." If the person makes an issue of it, allow them to go ahead of you. The two extra minutes you will wait are not worth an exchange of harsh words.

SALES STAFF COURTESY

Every hour on the job, you are the face of customer service for your company. That's a staggering responsibility, because you affect your company's bottom line. Poor customer service costs US businesses billions of dollars every year, because customers want a pleasant shopping experience and will go elsewhere if your store isn't providing it. Sixty-five percent of customers have completely cut ties with a brand over a single bad experience. Thirteen percent of customers who have a bad experience will tell at least fifteen people about it. Courtesy and respect, meanwhile, build customer loyalty.

Smile and make eye contact. This involves very little effort on your part, but it is a tried-and-true technique to improve your day and a customer's experience in your store. It's a fact that a smile will lead to increased sales.

Respect all shoppers. Check your attitude, prejudices, and other personal baggage with your coat when you clock in. Expect the best, not the worst, in people. Don't treat every customer like a potential shoplifter or a threat. We know you deal with some who are, but give the rest of us the benefit of the doubt. Use an honorific (Mr., Mrs., Ms., Miss) and last name when calling a customer by name, unless you know them very well or if they ask you to use their first name.

When creating your list of what's important when you're on the job, customers come first, second, and third. In other words, there isn't even a close second to customers when ranking what counts.

Now hear this! Please stop talking to coworkers and ignoring customers, and stop using your cell phone while on duty. (If you don't think your manager can see your phone under the counter, you're naive.) When you're out in cyberspace, you miss opportunities to smile at passing customers and to answer questions that they might have stopped to ask.

Be a good listener. Follow the active listening techniques outlined in chapter 2.

What's in a word? You're at work, not at the gym, so sound like a professional. Never say: "Huh?" "What?" or "Yea." And it's "*May* I help you?" not "*Can* I help you?"

Never say no immediately to a request. Listen attentively, repeat what the customer has said to indicate that you heard and understand the request, and then give your answer. If company policy is such that you cannot grant the request, state the policy politely, not defensively. If the customer insists, offer to consult a supervisor for a decision and do so. See chapter 2 for tips on dealing with difficult people.

Stop stalking. Don't stalk customers who decline your initial offer of assistance. It is annoying when you follow them around the store pointing out sale items or colors that you think look good with their hair. Read customer body language and watch for clues to determine if a follow-up will be welcome beyond your initial greeting.

No disappearing acts. Don't disappear during a sales transaction without explaining to the customer why you are leaving, approximately how long you will be away from your post, and why you must leave (you need to get receipt tape for the register, replenish shopping bags, find an answer to your question, or whatever it may be).

Peek-a-boo. Attention, clothing sales staff. Most customers don't appreciate it when you poke your head into their fitting room unannounced. Speak first from outside the space to let them know you're there to help.

Play favorites. Treat every customer as if they are your favorite, and you will be theirs!

CHECKLIST: Medical Manners Alert

A PATIENT IS RUDE IF

* he is late for an appointment;

* she misses an appointment without calling to cancel;

* he has not bathed or brushed his teeth immediately before an examination (or as close to the time of the examination as possible);

* she comes without a written list of questions for the doctor that will help to direct the discussion;

* she tears pages out of magazines in the waiting room; or

* he eats in the waiting area or examination room.

A MEDICAL PROFESSIONAL IS RUDE IF

* she keeps a patient waiting in the reception area for more than fifteen minutes beyond the time of their scheduled appointment or for more than ten minutes in an examination room without informing the patient of when they can expect the next step;

* he does not smile, make eye contact, and greet his patients warmly;

* her body language and listening skills indicate that her mind is not 100 percent on the patient;

* he has not reviewed the patient's medical history before beginning the consultation; or

* she fails to relate and empathize with patients.

FRONT DESK AND ACCOUNTING STAFF MEMBERS ARE RUDE IF THEY

∗ fail to smile, make eye contact, and greet patients;

∗ don't look up immediately when a patient approaches the reception counter, even if to say, "Good morning. I'll be right with you";

∗ fail to offer assistance to a patient who clearly needs it—filling out forms, hearing or understanding instructions, walking, getting up from a chair, opening a door;

∗ interrupt an in-person conversation with a patient to answer the telephone and have an extended conversation—the in-person conversation should take precedence over the call;

∗ gossip about patients, even without using specific names;

∗ discuss billing issues with patients in an accusatory manner;

∗ eat or drink in view of patients; or

∗ fail to keep current magazines in the waiting area.

MEDICAL OFFICE MANNERS
• •

People are in a medical office either to provide information and treatment or to receive it, depending on which side of the desk they sit on. Manners are what can help us meet in the middle and improve the experience for all.

Rx for Doctors You are stretched to the limit by your patient load and administrative demands, but make patients feel important when you're face-to-face. People protocol is as important as medical protocol.

Rx for Patients You don't feel well, but don't let your behavior inflict pain on the medical professionals who are trying to help you.

Rx for All If we examine and treat rudeness, maybe it will make all of us feel better.

ETIQUETTE OF WORSHIP

There are few communities on the planet today that do not have a rich diversity of individuals from many cultures blending socially and professionally. As our lives intertwine with people of different backgrounds and nationalities, often we share milestone moments in each other's lives—holidays, graduations, weddings, christenings, ordinations, and funerals or memorial services.

What is right when we attend a worship service in a faith that is unfamiliar? There are as many answers as there are faiths. We need only to demonstrate respect for the faith, the occasion, and our host, and the rest will fall into place.

The following rules will help you to prepare for an occasion in any house of worship, your own included:

Do Your Homework Prior to your visit, learn what you can about the religion and its protocol. Internet research is easy, and you can ask your host for information. Ask about schedule, attire, bringing children, order of the service, participation, offerings, and other details you will need to know before attending. Prepare!

Dress Code Ask your host about appropriate attire. Check to see if there is a dress code. Shoes removed? Heads covered? Hats removed? Arms covered? Most groups say "come as you are," but there are limits. Be discreet. We demonstrate respect when we dress appropriately.

Protocol In your conversation with your host or in your research, find out if there are gender-specific roles in the service or seating. Learn about the protocol of the service. It may include a processional, bowing heads, standing and kneeling, communion and other sacraments, blessings, call-and-response, singing, passing the peace, or a recessional. Most religions don't frown on a visitor participating in many of the rituals, but some are reserved for members of the faith.

Arrive Early Because you will have questions about where to sit and what to do, arriving early will give you the opportunity to speak with others.

Greeters Greeters are their congregation's best and brightest, so they will make you feel welcome when you walk through the door. They are a great resource for your questions. Smile and make eye contact. Wait to see if a handshake is offered. If it is, return it with enthusiasm. Introduce yourself and everyone in your group. Mention it if you are a first-time visitor.

Listen Practice active listening skills and be polite. Keep personal conversations with family and friends to a minimum, unless you are asking questions about the service.

Follow Others During a service, watch to see what others are doing and follow.

Children Brief children before attending a service so that they know what to expect and how to behave. Bring supplies for quiet activities that might divert a fussy child, but no food, beverages, candy, or gum. During the service, keep children quiet or leave the room and find a quiet area outside the sanctuary.

Exit There is usually a recessional, so once a service has concluded, wait to see what others are doing before you head for the exit.

After Thank your host for sharing the experience.

PARKING LOTS AND GARAGES

We learned about staying within the lines starting as early as kindergarten—coloring, classroom protocol, sports, and games—and there are innumerable occasions for us to rely on this training throughout our lives. So why is it that so many drivers fail to apply this concept when parking their cars in a lot or garage? Simple solution: each time you park, open your door, look down to see if you are within the limits of the lines, and, if necessary, adjust your car. Don't park so close to an adjacent car that it is difficult to open doors. Open your car doors carefully to avoid damage. Leave a note on a car you tap, ding, or dent.

To avoid break-ins, always lock your car and don't leave personal property inside if it can be seen through a window.

Respect the sacred parking law of the land: first come, first served. Don't try to dart into a space that another driver spotted before you did. For less stress and more exercise, try parking farther from your destination.

If you plan to dispose of the trash or cigarettes from your car, don't empty them onto the pavement of a parking lot or garage. Use trash bins at building entrances.

Check parking restrictions before leaving your car overnight or longer in a public parking lot or garage.

CHAPTER 4

FUN AND FITNESS

You may get time off for rest and relaxation, but your manners don't. Be sure to take them with you wherever you go to have fun and stay fit. In this chapter, we'll take a look at the role manners play in your leisure-time activities at the theater, gym, salon, and spa.

ENTERTAINMENT

THEATER AND PERFORMING ARTS

There is nothing more dynamic than live theater. How fortunate we are when we can have this experience. For a few hours, we become part of a microcommunity comprised of two groups, performers and audience, that find synergy when both sides play their roles effectively. It is important to remember that the energy in live performing arts travels in two directions. Not only are audience members receiving, but they are transmitting as well. While on stage, performers hear and see an audience and sense its tension and emotions, so noise and other distractions offstage can have a profound impact on what's happening onstage. Do your best to make sure that the performance you attend runs according to script.

Audience Handbook
Dress Code You're attending a live theater performance, so get excited and get dressed. But how do you know what to wear? Formal, informal? It's up to you. There is no official audience dress code in most theaters, but as Granny used to say, try to look presentable. Business casual is a good starting point, but you won't be tossed out for jeans and a windbreaker. Remember that theaters are notoriously chilly, so bring a sweater or jacket. And, ladies and gentlemen, please remove your hats—but not your shoes.

Take Your Seats Arrive no later than fifteen minutes before the published start time so that you don't have to climb over others as the house lights are dimming. If you're late, you will not be seated until there is a break in the performance.

If you are able, stand to allow others to pass you to reach their seats. If you have an aisle seat, step into the aisle to let others pass. As you enter a row, angle yourself so that your side or front faces seated row mates. No one likes a fanny in their face.

Mind your elbows, legs, feet, coat, and bags. Don't let them invade your row mates' space or protrude into aisles or rows in front or behind. No feet on the backs of seats in the row in front of you. If you are seated in a "bulkhead" seat, don't prop your feet on the rail or partition.

Performance Protocol Don't use a cell phone or other electronic devices during a performance for any reason. Management didn't mean everyone *except you* when they made their announcement to turn off or silence all devices, so comply. The noise and light from your screen are annoying to both audience and cast. And no cameras or recording devices.

Check the rules of a specific theater regarding food and beverage in the seats. No unwrapping candy, gum, or cough drops during a performance. Need to cough? Cover your mouth. Leave your seat if coughing persists.

Don't dig through a handbag or shopping bag during the performance.

Don't talk during a performance. If others around you are, it is OK to dispense a quick sh. If that doesn't solve the problem, call in the usher.

Barring an emergency, you should not leave a performance before it is over if you are seated in the middle of a row.

If you plan to attend with children, choose age-appropriate productions. Talk with tykes before you arrive to let them know what they can expect and what you expect from them: keep talking and questions to a minimum, no rustling paper, no kicking the back of seats, no standing in a seat, and that theater protocol mandates they stop in the restroom before the show (it's a best practice, so an acceptable white lie). Remove a child from the theater if he or she is approaching meltdown. An usher might help you find a seat at the back or allow you to stand somewhere.

MOVIES

The rules in the audience handbook above apply in movie theaters as well, although the dress code is much more relaxed. Come-as-you-are is the uniform of the day, and food and beverages are permitted, both within reason.

MUSEUMS, ART GALLERIES, AND HISTORIC BUILDINGS

Noise Don't talk during a tour or presentation. There are others in your group who want to hear the tour leader's narration. Some buildings are working office buildings, so keep voices low.

Respect the Tour Leader Listen and follow instructions. When you are engaged, the tour improves.

Cell Phones Many museums prohibit the use of cell phones in galleries. Check the specific policy of the site you are visiting.

Look, Don't Touch Yes, this rules *does* apply to you (even when no one is looking). Many objects are alarmed, and uniformed security will come a-runnin' to apprehend the culprit.

Photos Usually no photos are permitted, but check the policy of the site.

Stay with Your Group Wandering off from your tour group is a bad idea. You can get lost or enter areas that are off limits and alarmed.

Group Leaders and Chaperones Your job does not end when the tour begins. The in-house guide is not a babysitter or police officer. Supervise your charges.

HEALTH AND FITNESS

Establishing and maintaining a healthy lifestyle is something that smart people do. Because exercise and sports are important parts of that goal, a great deal of time is spent stretching, slimming, swimming, and sweating in the company of others. When next you pack your duffle bag to head to the gym, pool, golf course, or tennis court, tuck in manners and courtesy, and you and your fellow fitness force will have a more pleasant workout.

SWIMMING POOLS AND BEACHES

Cell Phones Use in moderation. Most people go to pools or the beach to get away from everyday stress and distractions. They don't want to share yours.

Lifeguards Help them do their job by leaving them alone. Fewer distractions for them mean increased safety for all. Respect guards when they ask you to do something. That something might be to leave the pool or the beach if you don't follow instructions.

Children Supervise children in and around a pool and at the ocean's edge. To be surrounded by running and screaming is not the reason that most of us go to a pool or to the beach. Noise dissipates more on a beach, but children still need to know that it's rude to disturb others. They should be guided not to run across the towels or blankets of others or to play so close to others that collisions occur.

Follow established pool rules for swim diapers and diaper disposal. Report accidents in the diaper department to pool management.

My Space/Your Space Don't walk on towels on the pool deck or blankets on the sand. So basic. And please, don't set up your gear so that you are joined at the hip with strangers. Anchor your belongings so they don't blow around in the wind.

Mind other swimmers when throwing balls in the pool or on the sand. If and when a ball hits you, don't be a grump.

Hygiene The sign says it all: "Shower before entering pool." Comply. Clean up after yourself and your children in the shower and changing room.

Too Much on View Consider the swim setting and dress accordingly. Are you swimming at a conservative country club pool, neighborhood swim club, or a singles party in your friend's backyard? One word of advice for wherever you may dip: *cover-up* (the noun). Have one with you at all times, read the territory, and wear it when appropriate. You only packed your speedo or microbikini and, oops, this is a family gathering or beach? Use it to cover up (now it's a verb).

Lap Lanes Respect lap lanes and the serious swimmers who exercise there. You may be at the pool for a fun day in the sun, but other swimmers are on a mission to swim rapidly and vigorously until on the verge of collapse. They won't take kindly to a volleyball to the head or horseplay in their lane.

Leave No Trace Secure your trash during your stay so that it won't blow away, and take all of it with you when you leave.

COUNTRY CLUBS

There is huge variation of rules and regulations relating to deportment and attire that private clubs and country clubs establish and monitor. Some clubs are very formal while others are informal, sporty, and laid back. When you join a club, you will receive a copy of the members' handbook, which defines conduct and etiquette. Follow the rules to show respect for the club and your fellow members.

When you visit a club as a guest of a member, ask your host for club etiquette tips or visit the club website for guidance on attire, clubhouse restrictions, golf course protocol, and tipping. To disregard club rules is disrespectful to your host and other club members.

Clubhouse Courtesy Use of cell phones and other electronic devices is usually permitted in designated areas, parking lots, and some outdoor facilities, but check the specific rules of each club. Smoking is usually permitted in designated areas.

Dress Code Check with your member handbook, member host, or the club website to get the answers you need. Determine which areas of the club you will be visiting, because the dress code varies from space to space.

Sample attire guidelines for a private club or country club may include:

Men
- shirts: sleeves and collared shirts at all times; tucked in
- shorts: Bermuda-length (walking shorts)
- golf: collared shirt tucked in; slacks or Bermuda-length (walking) shorts; approved golf shoes in designated areas
- hats, caps, and visors cannot be worn inside a clubhouse
- athletic wear not permitted in non-sports/fitness areas
- no denim, cargo shorts, or T-shirts in some clubs
- swimwear in pool area only

Women

- tops: no strapless or spaghetti straps unless evening formal wear
- golf: collared shirt tucked in; slacks, Bermuda-length (walking) shorts, or skirts; approved golf shoes in designated areas
- athletic wear not permitted in non-sports/fitness areas
- no denim, cargo shorts, or T-shirts in some clubs
- swimwear in pool area only

Golf Course Protocol The USGA (United States Golf Association) rules of etiquette serve as a guide for many country clubs, and additional club-specific rules may apply. Members follow the members' handbook, and visitors look to their host or the club website for guidance. Topics covered include:

- pace of play
- attire
- use of cell phones
- replacing and filling divots
- fixing ball marks
- raking bunkers
- tipping

SALONS AND SPAS

The professional in charge of your internal beauty is you, so check periodically to see if you need a manners makeover. But when your external beauty needs a tweak, update, or major overhaul, you are fortunate when you can turn to the pros in a salon or spa to get the job done.

Timing Arrive on time. When you are even fifteen minutes late, you disrupt the stylist's or attendant's schedule for the rest of the day. Call ahead if you are running late. Be prepared to wait politely when you do arrive late. Most likely, another customer has taken your time slot.

Need to cancel? Best practice is to call twenty-four hours in advance. Worst case, not later than thirty minutes before your appointment. This will allow the salon or spa to accommodate a walk-in in your place.

Holding Pattern You raced through your day to get to the salon on time, and now you sit for thirty minutes reading old magazines. Happens one time? Fine. Happens every time? Speak to the manager. Stay put and wait if you can; rebook your appointment if you can't. Either way, ask for a discount.

Hygiene Avoid strong perfumes and body sprays. Shower before a massage.

Quiet Time If sitting in a stylist's chair is the only me-time that you can carve out for yourself, you may not want to talk nonstop throughout your appointment. Quiet is OK, and if you don't want to jabber or be jabbered at, close your eyes after your initial conversation when you have discussed ideas for your service. Or read. Most stylists and attendants don't appreciate clients who spend a great deal of time on their cell phones.

Product Push Don't feel obligated to purchase additional products that are offered. Just say no! (Make that no, thank you.)

Yikes! Don't like the outcome? Most salons will offer a redo at no cost. This won't help if your hair is on the floor, so speak up early and often in the process.

Breaking Up Is Hard to Do Want to change stylist, manicurist, masseuse? If you have a long-term relationship, it is good manners to say goodbye in person or on the telephone; don't just disappear. You have no obligation to stay with anyone, so don't feel guilty. Just be courteous when you explain why a change is needed and leave the door open. Who knows, you may be back.

Tipping For a hair stylist, manicurist, spa attendant, and masseuse, 15–20 percent is standard. Give one or two dollars if you had a shampoo specialist wash your hair, or more if you received an extensive scalp massage or treatment. If you are using a gift certificate or discount coupon to pay, be sure to tip on the full amount of the service, not on what you are paying out of pocket.

CHECKLIST: Gym Etiquette

Apply the rules you learned on your elementary school playground when you go to the gym, and you'll earn a gold star: share and take turns, follow directions, don't show off, think of others, and play nice. Additional rules below will also help you to achieve that star:

* If you're sick, stay home. No amount of hand sanitizer will help others protect themselves from your germs (but let's all use it anyway).

* Exercise for the right reason. Are you there to stay fit, or do you want to show off your pecs or your exercise wardrobe?

* Speaking of spandex, don't forget decorum when it comes to your duds. Workout clothes may be scant but should provide strategic coverage and be clean and in good condition. And, yes, clothes come off in the locker room, but modesty should prevail.

* Do be concerned about personal hygiene before class, but limit perfume, cologne, and body spray, which can overpower a small space.

* Keep your eyes to yourself and conversation to a minimum. Working out is not a networking event or a singles mixer.

* Don't use your cell phone. Many people work out to escape the tensions of the outside world. No one wants to hear your conversations or a cacophony of ringtones. And about that cell phone on the floor next to your exercise mat . . . When it is set on vibrate and a call comes in, the floor shakes. Annoying! If you use your smart phone to log your workout or track your progress, silence it and place it out of the way.

* Don't hog the equipment. Adhere to the time limits set for use. Offer to rotate in and out when taking breaks from equipment.

* Don't invade the personal space of others. It is particularly important to leave a substantial perimeter when near someone using free weights or barbells.

* Offer assistance if others need spotting.

* Return equipment to its original location when you have finished using it.

* Use a towel to wipe down a machine after use, and put down a towel before sitting on benches or furniture when you're sweaty. Return towels to bins.

* Clean up after yourself in the locker room. Don't leave trash or your belongings behind. If lockers are available, don't park smelly attire there to fester for days.

* When taking a class, arrive on time. Don't talk to friends during class; it's distracting for all. Listen to the instructor. Respect the personal space of classmates. Don't set yourself or your belongings too close to others, and don't walk on someone else's mat.

* No, you do not own that particular spot on the floor in your cardio class. Don't ask someone to move if they claimed it first. If it is important to you that you work out in a specific spot, arrive earlier next time.

CHAPTER 5

MANNERS HIT THE ROAD

L et's go somewhere! There's nothing like travel to jump-start the body and the brain. New cities, new menus, new adventures, new friends . . . and new challenges. One tool to pack that will help to ensure a smoother experience for travelers anywhere on the globe is *courtesy*. Let good manners be your passport to a trip that is pleasant and memorable (in a good way). As a kind, courteous, and respectful traveler, you will improve not only your own experience but also that of your hosts and fellow travelers.

GETTING THERE

The challenges we encounter when traveling today include rudeness at many turns. You can't control the behavior of your fellow travelers, but you can control your own. Analyze what you are doing and how you can change to improve the travel experience for yourself and for everyone around you.

AIRPLANES

Below are tips and strategies for improving your travel experience when flying is your mode of transport.

They're at the Gate

At a crowded gate, don't put your belongings on empty seats that others could use. Keep your bags at your feet and avoid blocking aisles between seats.

Don't lie on the floor to sleep or practice yoga poses, and don't take off shoes and socks.

Dispose of trash you accumulate. Wipe up spills on seats and end tables.

Loud cell phone conversations are a pain to all. Headphones should be used with electronics. Don't hog power sources.

Don't contribute to the crowding in the boarding area while waiting for your group to be called. Stand aside so that individuals with group numbers that precede yours can pass freely.

Personal hygiene and public spaces are incompatible and should never meet. Find the nearest restroom to comb your hair; wash your face; apply makeup; clean, clip, file, or paint your nails; change a diaper; or dress a wound. Spotted recently was a pilot in uniform standing at the window of a gate flossing his teeth. Don't.

Security

Cooperate. The quickest way to be flagged for additional screening is to display an attitude. Screeners are professionals doing their jobs. Treat them accordingly. Listen and follow the rules.

Get organized. You *know* you'll be required to empty your pockets, dispose of beverage bottles, display personal items like toiletries, take off your shoes and belts, and unpack your laptop. Do some of these things as you approach the conveyor belt. Why wait until the last minute? The fewer things you carry, the better. Allow others to go ahead of you if you have children, multiple carry-ons, strollers, and such.

When you are cleared through screening, collect your belongings and move away from the conveyor belt to reassemble your gear.

Flying in Harmony

Yes, airline rules *do* apply to you. Turn off electronics when the announcement is made, not when a flight attendant has to ask you specifically to do so. Be quiet and attentive during the announcement on safety procedures. The information provided could save your life. Be respectful of flight crew and fellow passengers. A display of attitude at any altitude is sure to get you noticed, reprimanded, and possibly thrown off the flight. Drinking too much is often the root cause of bad behavior, so moderation is key. Problem with an unruly passenger? Ask the flight attendant for assistance. Don't challenge the offender yourself.

Recline when the lights go off. Simple and acceptable. With the current configuration of airline seats, you don't achieve a great improvement for yourself

OLD SCHOOL VS. NEW SCHOOL
Air Travel Evolution

Want to know what you missed? Ask an old-timer or baby boomer to describe how it used to be fun to fly. Passengers got dressed up, arrived at the airport a short time before their flight, checked their suitcase at the counter (no one carried luggage onto the plane in high heels or a three-piece suit), and got in an orderly line to board when their flight was called. They most likely had their ticket in hand before arriving at the airport, having obtained it from a travel agency or through the mail from the airline. A stewardess (yesterday's flight attendant) greeted them at the airplane door and offered them each a magazine, a menu, and a mint. Reaching their two-seat row, they introduced themselves to their seat mates, s-t-r-e-t-c-h-e-d out, and took a short nap before their full meal was served. Thirsty? They rang the call button for water. Sleepy? A pillow and blanket materialized. Inflight entertainment consisted of the aforementioned magazine and narration from the cockpit landmarks below. Meanwhile, back to the future, creature comforts when flying have all but vanished. Is it any wonder that today's airline passengers are stressed and surly?

when reclining your seat. So why not think about your fellow traveler and stay upright? If you do recline, don't do it suddenly or during meal or beverage service. Sitting in the penultimate row at the back? Think about the passenger in the last row behind you who cannot recline her seat, and don't drop yours into her lap.

Is there an extra seat in your row? It's not automatically yours. Offer it to your row mate, who may need it more than you do.

When boarding, don't stash your stuff in the first overhead bin you pass. The general idea is to use the space above *your* seat when possible, so try that first. Belongings stored under your seat should not spill over into your neighbor's space or block access in and out of your row.

Window shades up or down? Discuss among yourselves. They do not belong to the passenger in the window seat.

Table manners apply even at 35,000 feet, so use your napkin; don't chew, slurp, or burp loudly; and keep your elbows in. Be as neat as possible. Don't drink to excess. Carrying food onboard? Avoid foods with strong odors. It is a smart idea to carry sanitary wipes to clean your tray table before using it. Studies have shown that it is the dirtiest area on a plane.

Cover your mouth when sneezing and coughing, and use hand sanitizer often. This is a good rule even when you don't have a cold or flu.

Stand back from the luggage carousel until you see your bag. Offer to assist others with retrieving their bags from the belt. Supervise children when near the carousel.

Can We Talk?

Maybe not, if your row mate doesn't want to. As a courtesy, smile and say hello as you enter your seat, and then look for cues in body language to indicate if a passenger is open to a chat. If headphones go on as soon as cell phones go off, that's a clear indicator that your neighbor is closing the door to conversation. Respect his privacy.

Arm Rest-ling

The passenger in the middle seat is already at a space disadvantage, so yield both middle armrests to this individual. Case closed. The rest is easy: The passenger in a window seat uses the armrest there and leans in the direction of the window. The passenger in the aisle seat uses the outside armrest, and may lean a bit into the aisle, but keeps arms, legs, feet, and belongings from blocking the aisle.

Keep Your Eyes on Your Own Work

Reading over someone's shoulder—electronic or print media—is annoying, rude, and an invasion of privacy. Nothing to read? Better to close your eyes.

"Those" Children

Try to be kind and considerate of passengers who are flying with children. If they could make their child stop crying, don't you think they would? Children aren't equipped with an on-off switch. Parents have their hands full and don't need a grumpy passenger complaining loudly or sending dirty looks in their direction. Offer to help when and if you can. Consider swapping seats when you see that a family has been split up. It may be necessary for a parent to walk up and down the aisle in order to calm an unhappy baby. Deal with it.

If a problem develops because a parent is not supervising a child old enough to know better than to kick the back of your seat, scream at the top of her lungs, climb over you every ten minutes, or watch movies or listen to music without headphones, then speak politely to the parent. If a child in the row ahead is hanging over the back of a seat to make faces at you, a smile from you is sufficient. The parent may be trying to get the child to sit down. For problems that persist, enlist the help of a flight attendant, but try the polite, direct approach first.

The Facilities
Standing in line to use the lavatory? Think about yielding to a parent with a child or an elderly passenger. Emergencies take precedence. Be mindful of passengers seated in the rows near the lavatories while you are waiting in line.

Be sure to lock the lavatory door as soon as you enter. Don't embarrass yourself and others who may enter by mistake. Don't take too much time in the restroom. It is not the spot for a sponge bath or a complete makeup overhaul.

Wash hands thoroughly before leaving—at least twenty seconds is an effective wash, according to the Centers for Disease Control and Prevention. Leave the restroom clean when you finish. If you use paper to cover the knob when opening the door, don't let it fall to the floor; dispose of it responsibly.

Sleeping with Strangers
If you're planning to sleep, bring a neck pillow. The last thing your neighbor wants is your head on her shoulder. Don't fall asleep with your tray table down. Taking a sleep aid for a long flight? Request a window seat. Otherwise, it will be a problem for your row mates to climb over you when they need to leave the row.

Don't wear pajamas on overnight flights, even if you are flying first class or business class. Don't remove socks in any cabin.

You're Free to Move About the Plane
Yes, we're all concerned about deep vein thrombosis, but unless you have the aisle seat, getting up an unreasonable number of times during flight is disruptive to everyone in your row.

Try not to get up before your row mates have finished their food or beverages. And if one of them is sleeping, try to climb over them, if possible. Avoid pulling on the seat in front of you when you get up.

Let Me Off
The only reason you might have to get off the plane before people in the rows ahead of you is to catch a connecting flight. If so, let a flight attendant know your situation and mention it to passengers around you. Because you're special is not reason enough to be obnoxious and push past others.

TRAINS

1. See airplane rules starting on page 71.
2. Ground them.

TOUR BUSES

A tour bus is a community on wheels for the duration of a trip. Follow the rules, be a good neighbor onboard, and there will be fewer bumps in the road.

Before

Read and follow the tour company's code of conduct to the letter. Ask the tour company for tipping guidelines so that you will be prepared at the end of the trip.

During

Be on time for morning departures and when reboarding after activities. Don't make others wait for you.

Be friendly and courteous to all. A "good morning" is mandatory when it comes to travel manners. Read signals that others send through comments or body language. Some fellow passengers may not want to talk or interact. Throughout the trip, look for opportunities to help others who may need your assistance.

Respect the tour leader. Follow instructions and be attentive (or at least quiet) during narration.

Keep noise to a minimum in conversation and with electronics. If eating onboard is permitted, avoid pungent foods and contain your trash.

Hygiene is always a top concern when confined in tight spaces with many people. Avoid heavy scents of perfume or body spray, but do bathe regularly and keep your clothes clean. Do not remove shoes if you have foot odor, and never remove your socks. Don't comb or brush your hair; clip, file, or paint your nails; dry brush, floss, or pick your teeth. Always cover your mouth when you sneeze or cough, and use hand sanitizer often. If there is a restroom onboard, do your part to keep it clean when you finish using it.

Take Your Seats

Some companies will encourage passengers to rotate seats each day on an extended tour so that all passengers will experience the best views. If that is not mandated, think about setting up your own system, or at least don't take the best seat every day even if you get up earlier than others. Check behind you before reclining your seat, and recline slightly and slowly as you push back. Don't kick the seat in front of you, and don't pull on it as you get up from your seat.

Keep carry-on items tucked completely under your seat or in a storage rack overhead. Don't block the center aisle.

After
Take your trash with you when you leave the bus.

Exchange contact information with passengers who have become friends. Thank the driver and tour leader. Tip both to show your appreciation. The tour company will provide suggested guidelines, but tip within your means and to a level that reflects your satisfaction with the service.

CRUISES
Welcome aboard! You've just joined a floating community, and with membership comes responsibility. In other words, you are sharing the ship with up to four thousand new friends, and each of you has needs and expectations. Manage your expectations. Perfection should not be one of your must-haves. Before going aboard, say to yourself, "Things happen, and things work out." There. Your attitude is now seaworthy.

Dress Code
Check cruise literature for guidelines on attire. Most cruises are casual, but there are areas on the ship where a specific type of attire is requested—dining rooms, clubs, gyms, spas, and pools. Some cruises include formal evenings, but you may skip the festivities and fly below the radar on those occasions if you prefer. Try not to overpack. Storage space in passenger cabins and staterooms is limited, and there will be valet and self-service laundry and dry cleaning services on board.

Embarkation and Day-One Drill
Read your passenger handbook before leaving home, and follow the ship's rules and regulations to the letter. This will help to ensure that the embarkation process and the entire cruise will run smoothly for you and for those around you.

Be polite and respectful of crew members when you need to report problems or request a change of any kind. They are more likely to try to accommodate your request when you are patient and kind. This is a philosophy that you should follow throughout the cruise.

Wait your turn. You will be asked to queue up numerous times during the cruise for various reasons. Get used to it on day one, and be patient and polite.

Don't attempt to bring forbidden items onboard. It will slow down the boarding process for you and others behind you. Have all your documents in hand and ready for check-in. Step out of line if you need additional time to organize or check your belongings.

Label luggage with tags provided by the cruise line. Have a small carry-on for items you will need during the first few hours after boarding, because you may not be able to get into your cabin or stateroom immediately and your bags will not be delivered until later in the day.

Listen and follow instructions at the mandatory muster, aka the safety drill. It's not a game. Knowing where to go and what to do in an emergency can save your life. Skipping the muster is breaking the ship's laws.

Activities

If you sign up, show up. If your plans change, call to cancel so that your space can be filled by another passenger. Arrive at designated meeting spots at least ten to fifteen minutes before the advertised departure time. The crew, tour leaders, and other passengers don't wait for latecomers. Respect "adults only" activity requirements with minimum age restrictions.

Chair Diplomacy

Deck chair squatters, listen up. It is rude to park your belongings on chairs and walk away for extended periods of time. Give up the chair when you leave for a meal or other activity. It's just good manners to do so. Going to the theater with friends and family? Show up together. Don't send an emissary ahead to cordon off a row of seats. Plan to meet outside at a designated time and enter as a group.

Elevators

Don't push ahead of others waiting for an elevator, and don't overload cars. Want to avoid those long lines at elevator banks at peak times? Think about that all-you-can-eat dessert buffet, and hit the staircase every chance you get.

Noise

Noises carry on ships—in cabins, in hallways, and on balconies. Slamming doors, loud conversations, TV volume at the max, cell phones in the dining room, and electronics without headphones always show up on lists of passenger annoyances. Children running amok is another perennial complaint. The common courtesy that applies to cell phones on dry land also applies on the high seas.

SS *Germ*

Somebody always gets sick on a cruise ship. It's a given. Knowing this, you are wise to protect yourself and your family and friends by practicing preventative medicine. Be vigilant: wash hands for at least twenty seconds, use hand sanitizer often, cover your mouth when you sneeze or cough, and remain in your cabin when you are unwell. Most ships require that you report an illness of any kind to the ship's infirmary so that precautions can be taken to protect other passengers and crew members.

Buffets

Be patient when waiting in buffet lines. Repeat after me, "This ship will not run out of food." Don't do an end run around slower diners to snag your target item. Wait your turn, and then move quickly through the line. Slower diners, please think about stepping aside to let others pass.

Take small portions of food and return to the buffet if you want more, rather than wasting great quantities because your eyes were bigger than your stomach. Always leave your used plates at your table and get new plates when you return to the buffet. And no carryout please. Food is available onboard twenty-four seven, so you don't need that banana in your bandana.

Sharing dining tables on a cruise ship is an enjoyable experience and can lead to interesting discussions and new friendships. If you want to dine alone, go early or late to the buffet or book a private table in one of the dining rooms or restaurants.

(See additional rules on buffet dining in chapter 10.)

Disembarkation

Follow cruise-line instructions to the letter. Have a carry-on available with toiletries, medications, and clothes for the last night and final morning. Your luggage will be picked up while you are sleeping on your final night, and you won't be able to retrieve it until after you leave the ship the following morning.

Be prepared to wait in several lines. Have documents in hand as you approach checkout points. Step out of line and allow others to pass if you need additional time to locate an item. Patience and a smile are virtues and will serve you well.

Tipping

Some cruise lines include gratuities in passage fees because of staff rotation and variations in international tipping practices. For staff who served you for your entire cruise, it is kind and courteous to tip over and above these built-in gratuities.

- cabin stewards: $5–$10 per night
- dining-room server: $4–$5 per day
- bartender: $1 per round, more if you have a regular bartender
- room service: $2 per delivery
- spa services: 20 percent of the bill
- activity instructors: $5–$10 per service
- land tour operators: 5–15 percent of tour fee

SUBWAYS

Without some simple etiquette rules, subway travel would be chaotic in every way. Do your part to keep the peace and your sanity whenever you can. Look for codes of conduct signs in the system you are riding for culture and area-specific tips.

All Aboard

Queue to enter cars, and don't push in front of others who have been waiting longer than you. In a number of countries, professional pushers will do the job for you. Move to the center of the car when boarding and riders are standing. Don't block the doors.

Be aware that some countries designate subway cars for women only. Watch for signs.

No loud cell phone conversations, and wear headphones when using electronics. Don't read over someone's shoulder. Don't eat or drink on a subway car, and don't leave trash behind when you exit. There are bins in each station.

Take Your Seats

Offer your seat to others who may need it more than you do—elders, pregnant women, parents with babes in their arms, and passengers with disabilities. It's no longer a gender-based courtesy; it's need-based.

Don't put your stuff on an empty seat beside you. Keep legs, arms, and belongings out of the aisles. Remember that space you need to navigate without bumping into others includes the width of the luggage you are carrying, the backpack you are wearing, or the stroller you are pushing. Keep your knees together when sitting on a side-facing bench. Enough said.

Exiting

Let passengers exit the train before attempting to board. When planning your exit, begin to move toward the door after leaving the stop that precedes yours. Don't push to get through a crowd. "Excuse me" works remarkably well when you need to clear a path.

Stairs and Escalators

Don't block stairs. Stand to the right side on an escalator, and walk up or down on the left. Not everyone knows the rules, so a polite "excuse me" without attitude is all that is required to clear your path.

CARPOOL ETIQUETTE

Whether you carpool to work or to your favorite vacation spot, a few rules of the road will make your trips run smoothly. Defined rules and courtesy are good carpool partners.

Sharing Costs

Determine a fee structure. Is it based on gas, mileage, insurance, tolls, parking, maintenance? Is it split equally? How and when is money collected? Decide in advance.

Protocol

Establish a driving schedule. Be on time and determine grace period for latecomers (five minutes is standard for most carpools). What happens if the designated driver is ill or her car won't start, it breaks down, or she has to leave work early? The person who cannot drive on their assigned date has to make arrangements for a substitute.

Drivers must have insurance and should ask their provider about passenger coverage.

Determine your rules of the road covering food and beverage, use of cell phones, noise (radio, earphones), perfume and body spray, personal hygiene (grooming hair and nails, applying makeup), smoking, trash, bathroom stops, and other stops.

Create and distribute a roster of emergency contacts for all carpool members.

HOTEL HOSPITALITY

HOTEL HOW-TO

Hotel guests have high expectations when it comes to comfort, service, and amenities. But did you know that hotel management and staff have an equally long list of what they expect from hotel guests? Follow these guidelines, developed with input from hotel staff, and you will be voted a five-star guest:

- Wait your turn in the registration line. Every guest is a VIP to the hotel, not just you.

- Respect check-in and checkout times, but know that there is wiggle room on the part of the hotel. If you arrive early, the hotel may be able to store your luggage until your room is ready. Ask about late checkout. If the hotel is not full on the night you are checking out, you may be able to negotiate (or pay) for additional time.

- Don't bring a pet without making prior arrangements when you book the room.

- Keep noise and conversations to a minimum in public areas such as corridors and elevator banks.

- Have a request? Ask in a polite way, and it's more likely that it will be granted. Even complaints can be delivered courteously. Ask in person at the front desk for starters. Use "please" and "thank you" throughout your visit.

- Clean up after yourself. You don't have to clean the room, but you should attempt to contain the clutter. Treat the room and furnishings with care. If spills happen on carpets and bed linens, report them to housekeeping. Schedule a time when housekeeping can clean your room when you are out.

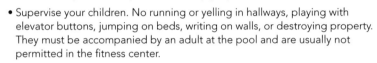

- Read and follow the house rules on linens replacement throughout your stay. Many hotels are going green and encourage you to reuse towels and will not change bed linens during a stay of under one week unless you request otherwise. No makeup on the towels.

- If you notice something in your room is damaged or broken, report it to maintenance immediately or you may be held responsible. If you break something, report that also. Unless it is obvious that you were deliberately destructive, your honesty will most likely get you off the hook.

- Supervise your children. No running or yelling in hallways, playing with elevator buttons, jumping on beds, writing on walls, or destroying property. They must be accompanied by an adult at the pool and are usually not permitted in the fitness center.

- Take only memories—and the complimentary travel-size toiletries—but not robes, towels, blankets, shams, hair dryers, hangers, ceramic coffee mugs, or other supplies that are cleaned for and reused by future visitors. Most hotels will add the cost of these items to your bill when they discover the theft. (Yes, that's what it is.)

B&B POLITE

Staying at a B&B translates to "welcome to our home." It's a more personal experience than using a hotel room, because you're staying in someone's residence. Proceed accordingly. B&B life is communal, so be on your best behavior.

- Book online whenever possible. Owners are busy twenty-four seven and not always near the telephone. If you do have to call, avoid breakfast hours and late-night calls. Leave a polite and detailed voicemail message; it will be your first impression to the owner.

- Follow the rules. Check the website for check-in and checkout times as well as policies about children, pets, and smoking. There may be a time frame for check-in. If you are running late, call ahead. The owner may be able to accommodate you.

- Respect the owner's personal spaces. Find out which rooms and areas are for guests and which are off limits and private.

- Read the signals of other guests. Most will be the type of people who want to chat with others, but some are not.
- Be neat—you are in someone's home. Report spills or damage immediately.
- Read and follow guest guidelines and the rules of the house.
- Keep your room clean and tidy. Don't rearrange the furniture.
- Children must be supervised, quiet, and told not to touch things.
- Report special needs when booking: dietary restrictions, accessibility concerns and needs, etc.
- "Please" and "thank you" go a long way.
- Had a pleasant stay? Ask the owner if he or she would like you to post a review and where.
- Leave a tip for housekeeping employees and a thank-you note for the owners at the end of your stay.

Since B&B's are known for their great breakfasts:

- Don't take too much food at breakfast buffet.
- Don't take food away without checking first with the owner or manager.
- Respect the schedule. Don't expect breakfast when you arrive fifteen to thirty minutes after the serving time.
- Let the owner know when you will miss a meal because of activities, etc.
- Avoid long conversations with the owner during breakfast. It's not the best time to ask for his or her list of the top-ten local spots for visitors.
- Tipping at breakfast is not appropriate.

CHECKLIST: Hotel Tipping

Think of travel and tipping as best friends forever, and try not to separate them. Many employees in the travel and hospitality industry rely on tips to supplement their salaried income, which is notoriously low. Below are general guidelines for tipping hotel staff during and at the end of your stay.

* **Front Desk Staff** not required

* **Doorman** not for merely opening the door, but for help with luggage ($1–$2 per bag) or finding a taxi ($2–$5, depending on how long it takes)

* **Bellmen** $1–$2 per bag or package delivery

* **Housekeeper** $2–$5 daily so that the tip goes to the staff member who provides the service

* **Concierge** not for a quick question answered, but for making reservations, $5–$10 at the time of service for simple tours or dinner reservations (more for securing hard-to-get theater tickets or other special services)

* **Food Service in Restaurant** 15–20 percent of the total bill

* **Room Service** check your bill to see if a 12–15 percent gratuity is included; if it is, you may wish to give another small tip ($3–$5) to the server who delivers your food and sets it up (if the bill includes a delivery fee, that is not the same as a gratuity and the server will not receive a portion of it, so adjust your tip accordingly)

* **Valet Parkers** $2–$4 when taking *and* returning your car

* **Maintenance Staff** not necessary to tip unless repairs are a result of something you have broken or have been provided immediately upon your request

AIRBNB

This is similar to a B&B experience, but your host may not be present during your stay. If that's the case, following the rules is even more important.

Guest

- Arrive and leave on time.

- Follow the house rules. Read them *before* arriving and again after you have settled in. If they don't cover all of the following, ask questions.

  - check-in and checkout times and procedures
  - extra visitors or guests (e.g., parties)
  - noise rules and quiet hours
  - children
  - pets
  - smoking
  - designated areas for eating

  - off-limits rooms or areas
  - laundry and supplies
  - kitchen and refrigerator
  - plumbing and electrical quirks or requirements
  - security steps and concerns
  - parking instructions
  - Wi-Fi rules and access
  - cleaning requirements

- If your host is on site, discuss schedules for kitchen, bathroom, and quiet hours in person.

- Don't rearrange the furniture.

- Spill something? Clean it up immediately and as thoroughly as you would in your own home. Break something? Follow the honor system and report it to your host immediately. Don't hope he or she won't notice. In either case, offer to pay for damages if you have not already paid a security deposit.

- Clean up prior to leaving, and dispose of trash.

- Tipping the owner is not required or expected. You may choose to tip a housekeeper or cook who supports your stay, if you wish.

Host

- Present a space that is clean, comfortable, and safe.

- Provide house rules and schedules before booking and again after your guests' arrival.

- Clearly define what supplies are provided: linens, towels, paper products, shampoo, conditioner, hair dryer, alarm clock, reading lamp, etc.

- Is anything off limits? Spaces, rooms, areas, supplies? Let your guests know.
- Be informative and reachable throughout the stay.
- If you will not be available, provide emergency contact information for a surrogate, caretaker, or neighbor as well as local service providers for repairs.
- Provide information on local activities, restaurants, and public transportation.
- The name "Airbnb" suggests food in some form or quantity, so tell guests what you will supply. Designate areas in the cupboard and refrigerator for guest food storage.

CHAPTER 6

COMMUNICATING COURTESY

Let's do our part to keep handwritten correspondence from dying. It's already on life support, a victim of technology! Email may be instantaneous and efficient, but it will never have the appeal, nor produce the pleasant effect, of a handwritten note or letter. Not only does handwritten correspondence convey your message, but it indicates that you cared enough to take the extra steps required to produce it. And yes, spelling counts, as do grammar and punctuation. These are use-or-lose skills, so work to keep yours from deserting you.

A good habit to cultivate is sending handwritten notes to friends, family members, and colleagues to congratulate them on an accomplishment or to share information that is of interest to you both.

THANK-YOU NOTES AND LETTERS

When you handwrite a thank-you note or letter, it is an obvious sign to others that you are a thoughtful, caring individual who appreciates the kindness of others. (A typed letter counts if your handwriting is illegible.) The note should be written promptly after a gift, service, or kind gesture is received and should include a specific reference to what was received. Points off for writing "Thank you for the gift" without mentioning the item.

YOU <u>MUST</u> HANDWRITE A THANK-YOU WHEN
- you receive a gift;
- you have been a guest at breakfast, lunch, dinner, or tea, or for an overnight visit;
- someone has shown you an extraordinary kindness or tribute;
- an individual has assisted you in some way;

- you receive an informational interview, mentoring, or a business referral; and
- you complete a job interview (maybe not *must*, but you *should* write it if you really want the job).

You may *email a thank-you* to a family member, close friend, or business colleague when there will be a delay in sending a handwritten note, or when thanking someone for providing information or assistance with a routine task, or when you meet for lunch or dinner on a regular basis and rotate picking up the check.

QUICK TIP
Thank You!

Poor ole "thank you." Saying it used to generate a "you're welcome" or a "my pleasure," but now seems to prompt a "no problem" more than anything else. People in the "no problem" camp defend their decision by saying theirs is a modest response to indicate that whatever they are being thanked for—service, favor, gift—was not an imposition or a hardship for them. So, let's give them a pat on the back for the sentiment, followed by a kick in the pants to stop. *Stop*, because "thank you" deserves better!

BUSINESS LETTERS

Knowing how to write a formal business letter is part of being a polished professional. Next time you are required to do so, reach for your own or your company's stationery, use the following template (or something close to it), and show that you know your way around business correspondence.

SAMPLE LETTER

Palmer Paper Company *[omit if your company name and address are printed on letterhead]*
678 State Street
Denver, CO 98531

March 15, 2017

Mr. John F. Lincoln
President
Green Enterprises
1234 Main Street
Burlington, VT 30983

Dear Mr. Lincoln: *[colons are used in business letters, not commas as in social correspondence]*

[Body of Letter]

[Wrap-up Paragraph]

Sincerely, *[or Sincerely yours, Respectfully, Respectfully yours, Warmly, With gratitude]*

[Signature—in black ink]

James L. Palmer
President
[email address optional]
[telephone number optional]

Enclosure(s)
CC: *[Name(s), if you are sending a copy to someone else]*

FORMS OF ADDRESS IN CORRESPONDENCE

Below is a brief introduction to formatting names and salutations in correspondence.

Name	Envelope	Salutation
Woman, married or single	Ms. Mary Logan	Dear Ms. Logan
Woman, married	Mrs. John Haynes or Mrs. Betty Haynes (if her preference)	Dear Mrs. Haynes
Woman, married uses maiden name (married to Jay Worth)	Ms. Mary Jones or to them jointly, Ms. Mary Jones Mr. Jay Worth	Dear Ms. Jones or Dear Ms. Jones and Mr. Worth
Woman, divorced	Mrs. Tina Proctor or Ms. Tina Proctor (if her preference)	Dear Mrs. Proctor or Dear Ms. Proctor
Woman, widowed	Mrs. Henry Wilson or Mrs. Carol Wilson (if her preference)	Dear Mrs. Wilson
Man	Mr. Walter Young	Dear Mr. Young
Doctor of medicine (MD), dental surgery (DDS), veterinary medicine (DVM), etc.	Ms. Janet Flint, MD Mr. Carl Grant, DDS (or for social correspondence: Dr. Janet Flint Dr. Carl Grant)	Dear Dr. Flint Dear Dr. Grant

Name	Envelope	Salutation
PhD	Ms. Janet Flint, PhD Mr. Carl Grant, PhD (or for social correspondence: Dr. Janet Flint Dr. Carl Grant)	Dear Dr. Flint Dear Dr. Grant
Protestant minister	The Reverend William Gaines	Dear Reverend Gaines
Priest, Roman Catholic	The Reverend Martin Evans	Dear Father Evans
Rabbi	Rabbi Jacob Allen	Dear Rabbi Allen
President of a college or university	Dr. Jane Ames President Tyler State University	Dear Dr. Ames or Dear President Ames
Mayor of a city	The Honorable James Smith The Mayor of Omaha	Dear Mayor Smith or Dear Mr./Madam Mayor
US senator	The Honorable William Harper	Dear Senator Harper
State senator	The Honorable Harold Moore	Dear Mr. Moore
US representative or state representative	The Honorable Sarah Collins	Dear Ms. Collins
Judge	The Honorable James Franklyn	Dear Judge Franklyn

WORDS OF CONDOLENCE

When extending condolences to family, friends, or colleagues, often it's what you don't say that matters more than what you do say. Choosing the wrong words can add to someone's pain, but getting in touch to say you care and want to help is more important than semantics. A condolence message should not be delivered through voicemail, email, text, or social media. Call, visit in person, or write a heartfelt note on stationery or a greeting card.

Reaching Out

Say something, anything. No contact means you don't care or demonstrates that the situation is more about you than the bereaved—you're too uncomfortable, busy, or unsure of what to say, so you say nothing.

If you ask someone, "How are you doing?" listen to their response. Their first answer will probably be, "Fine. I'm OK," which lets you off the hook. Who wants a difficult discussion, right? Wrong. Instead say, "I hope you are taking care of yourself. Are you able to sleep/eat/work?" Then offer specific assistance, based on their response. Be a good listener. Don't ask too many questions about the circumstances of the illness, accident, or death. Wait to see if information is forthcoming.

Stay in touch. Check back at regular intervals to see what is needed. Call or write at holidays and on anniversaries of the death, both of which will be particularly painful for the family and loved ones of the deceased.

It's never too late to get in touch. There will be a flurry of cards, notes, and calls immediately after a death. Then they stop. To receive something later will not be a painful reminder, but rather an indication that someone still cares. And don't be afraid of talking about the deceased because you think you don't want to remind someone of their loss. They are living with it every day.

Share personal memories or stories. Find photographs to copy and give to the family.

When you lose a business colleague and don't know their family members, address a card or letter to the closest relative. The family will appreciate hearing about your working relationship with their loved one. When a friend loses a loved one whom you did not know, send a note to the friend to say that you are thinking about her.

How to Help

"Let me know if I can do anything" is an empty offer. Someone who has just suffered a tragic loss is not likely to call to ask you to pick up their black dress from the dry cleaners. But if you call to say you will be running errands and you want an assignment, they might accept your offer. Or call to say, "May I come by to help get the house ready for your guests?" or "I'm going to the grocery store. Let me pick up what you need," or "I'm free on Monday. If you have things to do to prepare for the service, I can stay with the children/answer the phone/walk the dog."

After the funeral, call again with a specific offer: "I would like to help you with thank-you notes," "Let me pick you up tomorrow for lunch or errands." Then, when you're together, be a good listener. You don't have to have the perfect words or all the answers. You just have to be there and listen. Call soon to offer again if your first offer(s) are refused.

Gifts

Flowers at the time of a death say you are thinking about someone's loss, but they can often be overwhelming in number and become a burden when they have to be moved or distributed. Instead, send flowers or a plant a week or two later to someone's home, or, better yet, deliver them in person.

Gifts of time and talent are also appreciated: food that can be frozen, a gift certificate for home-delivered meals, airport transport for out-of-town mourners, housecleaning before mourners arrive, addressing thank-you notes, babysitting, or running errands. Or wait and offer your gift of service a week or two after a funeral when everyone else disappears.

What Not to Say

Well-meaning family and friends often rely on what they think are tried-and-true phrases when extending their sympathy in writing or in person. Some of these phrases are completely inappropriate:

- *I know how you must feel.* You don't.
- *He/she is in a better place.* That's not for you to say.
- *It's God's (or another deity's) will.* Not helpful, and the recipient may not share our religious beliefs.
- *I know this is a tough time for you.* Inadequate understatement.

- *You'll feel better soon.* You can't predict the timeline for someone's grieving.
- *You will get through this and be stronger on the other side.* You don't know this.
- *It was a long ordeal; you must be relieved.* A hurtful comment; you can't assume that someone feels relief, no matter how difficult the period leading up to the death.
- *You must start to move on with your life.* Presumptuous comment.
- *(The deceased) would not want you to . . .* It's not your place to tell someone what their loved one would think or feel.
- *This is like when my aunt died last year. . . .* No comparisons or turning the conversation to other tragedies. This trivializes the loss that you are supposed to be addressing.

Instead Say

Say something more generic that indicates your concern, followed by active listening or sharing a personal memory of the deceased.

- *I'm sorry for your loss.*
- *I want you to know that I am thinking about you and would like to help in some way.*
- *I don't know what to say; there aren't any words.*
- *Nothing I can say will make the pain go away, but I offer my love and support.*
- *I cannot begin to understand what you are going through or feeling.*
- *This must be so very hard for you. I hope I can help in some way.*
- *He was such a good person and made a lasting impression on so many people.*
- *It was an honor to have known her.*
- *I will always remember what a kind and gentle person he was.* (Then share a story or memory.)
- *Sending our prayers and a hug.*

Think more about warmth than words, and a short visit to talk is better than any call or card. Call ahead to schedule; don't drop in.

Condolence Thank-Yous

Thank-you notes are required when you receive a personal letter of condolence, flowers, gifts, services, or donations to a charity or cause. Commercial sympathy cards with the sender's signature only don't require a thank-you note, but it is good to mention them to the sender when you see them next. Preprinted thank-you notes provided by a funeral home should be personalized with a short note. Addressing and mailing these is a job for someone who has offered their help.

GRAMMAR REVIEW

Your knowledge of spelling and grammar is an important part of your brand. Each time you write a document, note, or business email, your proficiency—or lack of it—is on display. You don't have to be a grammar geek to write successfully, but you do need to demonstrate that you have a basic command of the English language. Don't let common grammatical errors tarnish your brand.

Provided here is a quick grammar tune-up. Follow it up with a major overhaul if you feel that you are challenged in this area. There are numerous resources available in libraries, bookstores, and online.

PARTS OF SPEECH—THE CAST OF CHARACTERS

- **noun** person, place, or thing; singular or plural
- **verb** usually an action or occurrence
- **pronoun** takes the place of a noun (I, he, she, they, you, me, him, her, they, you, it)
- **adjective** modifies or describes a noun or pronoun
- **adverb** modifies a verb, adjective, or other adverb, preposition, phrase, or clause

Supporting Players

Several common grammar mistakes are addressed in the information below.

Incomplete Sentences A sentence consists of a subject and verb. It is a complete thought, not a fragment.

- Incorrect: He lost the primary election. Probably because of poor performance by precinct workers.
- Correct: He lost the primary election. Many say it was because of poor performance by precinct workers.

Run-on Sentences Two or more phrases or clauses that can stand alone must be fused with a proper connector.

- Incorrect: We're running late, meet me at the car.
- Correct: We're running late, so meet me at the car.

or

- We're running late. Meet me at the car.

Subject-Verb Agreement Both the noun and the verb describing it must be singular or both must be plural.

- Singular subject and verb: *The dog runs.*
- Plural subject and verb: *Dogs run.*
- Singular subject (one company, a collective noun): Ben & Jerry's is located in Vermont.
- Plural subject (two people): Ben and Jerry make ice cream.

Comma vs. Semicolon Commas and semicolons are used to punctuate a series within a sentence. Use semicolons when the items in a list themselves contain internal punctuation.

- *I ordered copy paper, toner, and cleaning supplies.**
- *We picked new laptops for IT; desk conversion kits for HR; breakroom supplies including coffee, tea, and milk; and a new fax machine for R & D.*

Serial Comma A lively debate has been going on for some time about whether or not to use a final comma been the last two words or phrases in a series (e.g., after "toner" in the sample sentence above). Many writers feel that the final comma is needed if there is any chance that the information included in the series will be misinterpreted, and it is the standard style for most American book publishers. Newspaper publishers, however, do not use serial commas.

Misplaced Modifiers
- Incorrect: <u>At seventeen</u>, my mother started to take me on college visits.
- Correct: <u>When I was seventeen</u>, my mother started to take me on college visits.
- Incorrect: Please bring me a <u>hot</u> cup of coffee.
- Correct: Please bring me a cup of <u>hot</u> coffee.

PRONOUN AND VERB AGREEMENT

Subjective pronouns take the place of a noun (person, place, or thing), and are the subject of a sentence or clause: *I, he, she, they, we, you* (did something…).
- ***She*** *coordinated the charity bazaar.*
- ***They*** *traveled to Turkey on business.*

Possessive pronouns show ownership: *mine, his, hers, theirs, yours, ours.*
- *The new house would be* ***theirs*** *at the end of the month.*
- *Which document is* ***yours***?

Objective pronouns are objects of a verb or a preposition: *me, him, her, them, us, you* **(something was done** *to* **or** *for* **them, not** *by* **them).**
- Object of a verb:
  - *The director <u>chose</u> me to sing the opening number.*
  - *The cadet corps <u>saluted</u> them at the end of the parade.*
- Object of a preposition:
  - *Mary threw the ball <u>to</u> me.*
  - *The teacher received a letter <u>from</u> her.*
- Often, saying pronouns out loud in various contexts can help you select the right one:

  Mary threw the ball to____ ?
  - *me* (not *I*)
  - *her* (not *she*)
  - *them* (not *they*)

PRONOUN PITFALLS

A. Use the following test to determine the correct <u>objective pronoun</u>.

Which sentence below is correct?

- *Send the email to Judy and I, and we will respond.*

or

- *Send the email to Judy and me, and we will respond.*

The quickest way to determine if your pronoun is correct in a sentence with a compound (more than one) subject is to omit the other subject and say the sentence using only the pronoun in question:

Incorrect: Send the email to ~~Judy and~~ **I.**

Correct: Send the email to ~~Judy and~~ **me.**

Therefore the original sentence is correct, as follows:

- *Send the email to Judy and **me**, and we will respond.*

B. Use the same test for sentences using <u>subjective pronouns</u>:

Which sentence below is correct?

- *Judy and me will represent the Foster Agency at the meeting.*

or

- *Judy and I will represent the Foster Agency at the meeting.*

We'll remove poor Judy once again, and test the results to show the correct usage.

Incorrect: ~~Judy and~~ **me** will represent the Foster Agency at the meeting.

Correct: ~~Judy and~~ **I** will represent the Foster Agency at the meeting.

Therefore the original sentence is correct, as follows:

- Judy and **I** will represent the Foster Agency at the meeting.

COMMONLY MISSPELLED AND MISUSED WORDS

Effect Noun. A change that results when something is done or happens.
- *His harsh words had a bad **effect** on everyone present.*

Affect Verb. To produce an effect upon something.
- *The stroke **affected** her speech.*

Advise Verb. To give an opinion or suggestion.
- *He **advised** her on financial and legal matters.*

Advice Noun. An opinion or suggestion.
- *Please give me your **advice** on how to proceed.*

It's A contraction of the words *it* and *is*.
- ***It's** going to be a cold winter.*

Its The possessive form of *it*.
- *The store was required to fix **its** elevator.*

You're A contraction of the words *you* and *are*.
- *You can't learn if **you're** not in class.*

Your The possessive form of *you*.
- *Bring **your** book when you come to class.*

They're A contraction of the words *they* and *are*.
- *Let me know when **they're** in the neighborhood.*

There A location.
- *Put the sofa over **there.***

Their The possessive pronoun for *they*.
- *She is **their** mother.*

CHAPTER 7

GOING SOCIAL

I t's a given that the Digital Age is here to stay. But don't let anonymity or the fact that you are behind a screen mask the courtesies that you would grant in face-to-face interactions. In fact, these courtesies become even more important as we are not able to rely on cues, such as a smile, a touch, or a gentle voice for direction. When in doubt, err on the side of kindness. Guidelines for various social media are outlined below.

CELL PHONE COURTESY

Handheld cell phones have been in use for decades now, and while advances in their design and technology move at breakneck speed, the etiquette governing their use has not evolved at a similar pace. As we did in the early days, we're still dropping everything when a call comes in and shouting, "CAN YOU HEAR ME?" No progress there. Cell phones play such a prominent role in our lives today, from good tool to bad influence, that you will find courtesy tips regarding their use tucked into every chapter in this book. The additional information below will help polish your personal code of conduct when it comes to using your phone.

R U RUDE? Cell Phone Courtesy

Let's take a look at where and when things go wrong when cell phones are in the picture.

R U RUDE?	CORRECTIVE MEASURES
While in conversation with someone at a business conference, networking event, or party, your phone rings and you check the display, determine you are not going to answer the call, put it back in your pocket, and resume your conversation.	RUDE. Unless you are a first responder, CEO of a Fortune 500 company, or designated driver for a pregnant woman, you do not need to interrupt a face-to-face conversation to text, answer an incoming call, or even check the display, especially when speaking with a new acquaintance or business contact. Voicemail and texts have you covered. Allow them to do their jobs and you to do yours, which is to focus on the person you're with, not on anyone or anything in the virtual world. If you are expecting a critical call, tell your companion, and excuse yourself when it comes in.
You always place your phone on a conference table or dining table, but it's in silent mode.	RUDE and egocentric. Placing a phone on a conference table or dining table is like announcing to those convened that you think you are very important, you hope this meeting or meal will be worth your time, and that you may need a diversion because you're on the verge of boredom already. Turn off a cell phone when entering a meeting or sitting down to dine, place it out of sight and forget it. If you feel the urge to check your messages to see if that call came in from the White House, Downing Street, or the Kremlin, excuse yourself from the table for a short period of time. Don't do this more than once during a gathering.
You routinely take cell phone calls at your desk at work.	RUDE and embarrassing. You probably didn't even realize that your coworkers were staring at you, mouthing the word *loud* to one another. Why is it that we raise our voices when speaking on a cell phone (studies say two to three times louder than when speaking face-to-face)? Maybe it's a throwback to our first portable communication device, the can on a string? No, it's in fact because we lose our tether to the real world when we begin to walk and talk in cyberspace. Now that you know this will happen, move away from others when you speak on your phone.

R U RUDE?	CORRECTIVE MEASURES
No one knows you on public transportation, so it's OK to talk about anything you like in a catch-up phone conversation with a family member or friend.	RUDE and TMI. We don't want to hear about your foot fungus, twelve-hour labor, or make-up sex. How do you know what's fit for a phone conversation in a public place? Take the cringe-worthy test to decide: Would you talk about it in detail at a dinner party with new acquaintances? If not, then change the subject when in public. *Please!*
Several times during a networking event, you step behind a potted palm to respond to text messages.	RUDE and foolish. We see you in the fronds, and now we know you're not really engaged in the event. The outside world is more interesting to you than we are. Don't lose opportunities to connect with people in real time because your focus is in the virtual world. Be here.
In a theater, a person in the row in front of you has been texting for the first ten minutes of the movie. You decide to move to another seat instead of saying something to the offender.	RUDE, the texter, not you. You did the right thing. Courteous people don't correct the rude behavior of others. In fact, it's rude to do so, and can be dangerous. But this behavior is more than rude; it breaks the rules of the theater. You should notify management and let someone from the staff deal with the offender.
You're a proud multitasker, and your phone makes it possible to work wherever you are. What's not to like?	RUDE and sad. To the parent walking home from school with your child after a long day apart; to the family sitting together at dinner in the glow of four electronic devices; to the friends out for an evening to catch up and reconnect, *put down your phones.* Those are precious times together, and you're not there.
You use your phone in the car for calls or texts, but only when stopped at a traffic light.	RUDE and illegal. I was one of the six people in line behind you this morning who missed the light. We were inconvenienced, but I guess you and your virtual buddy were good. And admit it, the last few words of your text were typed after you started to drive, endangering everyone in your path. Note that things aren't much better when you use your hands-free phone while driving, because your focus is on your call, not on the road.
It is OK to be on your phone while standing in line at the deli to order, as long as you stop talking to answer questions from the counter attendant as you order and pay.	RUDE on so many levels. Both the counter attendant and the person on the other end of your call are dangling as you ping-pong between you, and the people behind you in line wait additional time because you lose your train of thought and have to reread the menu or ask "how much?" again.

TEXTING

Those who analyze social trends warn that texting is contributing to the loss of the ability to communicate face-to-face, because, more and more, users allow it to take precedence over conversations in real time. The informality of texting has led us to believe that there are no hard rules, and, therefore, there can be no offenses. But the texting community has begun to take notice of bad manners and annoying behavior, so below are some tips for a texting code of conduct. Take a look at your manners to see how they measure up.

WHO

Identify yourself in the message when texting someone for the first time.

Know your audience. Who is primarily a texter, and who responds by email only? You're the one who needs to adapt to your audience each time you send a message.

Group texts can be annoying, so handle with care. Everyone in a group may not need to receive every message sent to other members. Remember that when you reply to a group message, you are automatically replying to all.

WHERE

Please stop texting in theaters, concerts, restaurants, meetings, church, public restrooms, or when you should be paying attention to real-time people and experiences.

Remember that text messages aren't always private. Put your phone down on the table or desk for a minute, and anyone in the vicinity can see the first few lines of your incoming messages, by mistake of course. Most phones will allow you to choose whether or not a preview of incoming texts appears. Check your settings to see if you can turn that feature off.

WHEN

Don't text when in face-to-face conversations with others, unless you explain what and why you are doing so.

A text is not an appropriate way to communicate serious concern, condolences, or thanks.

WHY

Return a text message with a text, not a call, because it is the initiator's preferred method of communication at the time the message was sent. When you initiate contact with someone, you can choose the communication method. Texting may be the best way to get the attention of the individual who lives by text and ignores email and phone calls, but it's not everyone's first choice.

HOW

Keep messages short, and decide when you can relax into txt spk and when you need to channel *The Chicago Manual of Style*. For most users, somewhere in between will be comfortable and appropriate. For work-related texts, move the formal/informal needle in our brain to the formal side.

Annoyed by autocorrect? You can turn it off by changing your settings. Make sure that your spell checker is turned *on*. And, as with email, a message typed in all capital letters is interpreted as SHOUTING. Emojis are not a bad thing. They can help clarify your messages if not overused. Proofread your message and double-check the recipient before hitting send.

HOW FAST

Don't assume that everyone will answer your message in a nanosecond. Savvy texters have a life outside their phones and the good sense to know when and where to use technology. Sending follow-up texts to affect a response is annoying.

HOW LONG

Too many messages to one individual can feel like stalking. Don't send multiple texts to elicit a response.

Try to sense when it's time to end a conversation and sign off. Back and forth "yup," "k," "Ha!" or five-minute pauses? It's time. It's rude to disappear in the middle of a text conversation, so give an obvious sign-off.

SOCIAL MEDIA

Billions of users have discovered the pleasure and benefits of creating and belonging to virtual networks that allow them to share information and ideas from their personal and professional lives. But just as it is important to exhibit courtesy and kindness in the real world, members of social media communities must recognize the need to promote these qualities in the virtual world. Hold yourself and your virtual cohort accountable for inappropriate behavior. But how do you know what is or is not acceptable content? By using the following litmus test: Don't

post or tweet anything that you don't want your mom to announce at Thanksgiving dinner, your neighbor to share on the community listserv, or your boss to post on the company bulletin board. Here is a quick look at some of the most popular social networking sites and related etiquette.

FACEBOOK

Your posts should reflect your everyday life with its ups and downs, a window through which your family and friends can glimpse of your life, warts and all. Virtual you should be an alter ego to real you, not an invented character with an imagined life. Be kind, ethical, empathetic, and, above all, genuine. Share opinions, yes, but without frequent rants or criticism and always in a respectful manner.

Filter Don't say anything on social media that you would not say in person in a face-to-face conversation. The anonymity of the virtual world has brought out a dark side of many people. Unless you are behaving badly in person, and we know you're not, don't gossip, bully, shame, or insult anyone on Facebook or other social media sites. Don't criticize, and don't post when you're angry, wounded by someone's comments, or strongly disagree with something you read. Wait. Think. Draft. Think some more. Reread. Post. And stop complaining. Recent studies indicate that it's not healthy for you. We have known for a long time it's not healthy for those around you.

Friending and Unfriending There should be a reason to link, and those reasons are numerous, but just to increase your numbers should not be one of them. And it's OK to unfriend. If you have been out of touch for some time or your interests or circle of friends have changed, there may not be a reason to stay connected. If you don't want to unfriend someone but can't stomach another cat video or Candy Crush update, hide the person from your feed.

Who R U? Receive a friend request from a stranger with no accompanying message? Before accepting it, click on the profile to find out if you have anything in common. It's OK to ignore it if you see no connection. It may be from someone who is looking to increase their numbers and found you through links to others.

Oversharing Don't make every post about you. Your friends care, but they don't want to hear intimate details of your health, love life, or lapses of judgment. And do they really need to know/hear/see
- the last five articles you read;
- recipes you want to try;
- where you're having dinner on a Tuesday night (although if that dinner is in Acapulco, then maybe . . .);
- that you just checked in for sedation dentistry;
- that you took 150 photos at SeaWorld, and here they are; or
- another self-portrait or political rant?

Tag Ask permission before tagging people in photos. If the friend is job hunting or was supposed to be at home in bed with the flu when barhopping with you, they might not appreciate your sharing their whereabouts. If you're tagged and wish you weren't, you can unlink a photo of yourself and then ask the poster to remove it. It is possible to adjust your settings so that you can manually review all photos of you before they are posted.

Be Generous and Grateful Say thanks often, and credit sources when reposting and sharing.

TWITTER

Twitter, the haiku of communications platforms, gives us 140 characters to get our message across. Some say it has made better writers of us all, but that is debatable. What everyone can agree on is that Twitter, which began as a method for small groups of friends to communicate in real time, has grown to a global social-networking phenomenon embraced not only by individuals but also by organizations, businesses, and governments.

Condense It On Twitter, we are forced to condense our content, but unlike some canned soup, our hearty ideas don't get watered down. We have to convey an entire thought or opinion in 140 characters, often with links to supporting evidence or background information.

Filter It Be genuine and kind. Don't post anything that you would not say to someone in face-to-face conversation. And always think *R-E-S-P-E-C-T*. It's OK to share your opinions, but respect the opinions of others. Rein yourself in on rants and complaints, and cyberbullying is a dreadful disease. Don't catch it.

Master It It's not all about you, or it shouldn't be. For every tweet that promotes you or your agenda, send out four or five that provide useful information or applaud someone else. Tweet with care. Others can share or repost your tweets and add their own comments or spin.

Hashtags are useful for organizing topics and tracking discussions but can be overused. Three or fewer in a tweet is the suggested max by Twitter gurus. You don't want to be branded as a #spammer.

Follow It? Don't think, "Tweet for tat." You don't have to follow someone just because they follow you. If you decide to unfollow someone, don't publicly announce it. Don't follow someone with the goal of encouraging them to follow you as a method to increase your numbers, and then immediately unfollow them.

Protect It Consider setting up a private account or making adjustments to your settings. The Protect My Tweets setting will prevent people who are not following you from reading your tweets (but know that many users don't like following people who opt for this setting). Disabling the Tweet Location feature also increases your privacy, and you can re-enable it at times when you want your friends to know where you are when tweeting. Don't share your phone number or email address on Twitter.

LINKEDIN

The LinkedIn network that you build should be a group of legitimate professional connections. It's not a numbers game, nor is it Facebook dressed up. It's about people supporting one another professionally to build their brand online. When you reach for LinkedIn, think of it as going to work in cyberspace.

Look the Part Use a professional photo when creating your profile. Your profile and posts are often your first impression in the virtual business world. Spelling counts, as do grammar and punctuation.

Sound the Part Swearing and personal criticism are nos. When asking for something, use the same courtesy that you would if dealing with an individual in person. Set limits for yourself on how often to post. More is not better, it's just more. Post one or two times a week, but *never* more than once a day.

Protect Your Brand Don't include your email address in your profile. When editing your profile, turn off the Notify Contacts feature to keep edits private. You can turn it on again when you finish and when you have news to share. Remember that people are notified when you view their profile. When others view yours, it's OK to follow up with them, but not immediately.

Connecting It's a good idea to customize your invitations. Tailor them by requesting to connect on the profile page of your target individual. Include a personalized message, such as a reminder of where and when you met or a congratulatory message addressing something that they accomplished. If you choose to use the auto-template feature People You May Know, include a personal note.

It's OK to send an invitation to connect quickly after meeting someone face-to-face. It's not considered stalking, just smart use of the medium, but wait a few days before reaching out. If you request to connect with someone you don't know—a recruiter or resource in your field—do so with a personalized message and information about yourself. Don't resend an invitation multiple times. LinkedIn has an auto reminder, so if you resend, the target individual will be bombarded by requests from you and will likely become annoyed.

Before accepting an invitation to connect, check the person's profile to see what you have in common. If you accept, respond with a short note. It's OK to ignore a connection request if, after viewing the requestor's profile, you see no reason to connect. When it's time to weed your network, it's OK to remove connections. They won't be notified.

Help Others This is the number-one rule of networking and a primary focus of LinkedIn. Give more than you expect to get. Post articles that are relevant and helpful to your industry, start discussions on relevant topics, or send specific information to particular contacts. Keep contacts fresh. Acknowledge updates (new positions, promotions, etc.) with a short note, but use good judgment. Not every update needs a "Congrats!" with a happy face. Participate in discussions. Share information that may help others, as either a broadcast or targeted messages.

Endorsements Don't sprinkle endorsements like grass seed. If you have first-hand knowledge of the skills and abilities of a connection, you are free to endorse. Provide specific information whenever you can. It is neither necessary nor expected that you will reciprocate when you receive an endorsement.

When asking for endorsements, target people who know you and your work. Send a customized message and include sample text or examples of your work that could be cited in their endorsement. Thank people for their endorsements if they are sincere and the endorsement is accurate.

Groupspeak Check group guidelines before asking to join. They are not marketing tools. You should have legitimate information to share with group members to justify your joining.

INSTAGRAM

Instagram, the app for sharing photos and videos, is not meant to be a moment-by-moment chronicle of your life if you are trying to build a wide following. Think greatest hits, not the complete songbook. But if your primary goal is to stay connected with friends and family, however, using it as a daily diary is a good approach.

Find Your Voice Nobody wants to see your version of someone else's photo style or content. Post original material. Don't be a copycat.

Social To get the most out of Instagram, think two-way street. Follow your favorite photographers, and comment and engage in conversations. "Like" is fine, but a comment is better. It is not necessary to like every photo you see. Hold out for outstanding. Honest interactions will lead to building a larger network.

What Am I Looking At? Posting an extraordinary photo? Provide some background—the who, what, where, when, and why you took the shot. Tell a complete story.

Credit Your Source If someone helped you take a photo or was inspiration for it, give credit to them with their Instagram handle in your comments.

Oversharing Change your mind-set if your philosophy is "if one is good, ten is better." Instead, think quality over quantity. We can see that you like sunsets, but what else have you got? Sunsets alone will not build a network.

#HashtagOverload Planning to include a string of hashtags? Place them at the end of your caption or in a comment so that they are out of the way when reading what the photo is about.

Wider Distribution You can link Instagram to your Twitter account when you use your same user name for both. But do you need to cross-post every photo?

CHAPTER 8

BE OUR GUEST

The good news first: Your personal and professional lives are filled with parties, celebrations, receptions, lunches, dinners, teas, reunions, and other assorted gatherings. The bad news next: Your success as a host or guest at these events teeters on your knowledge of the etiquette of entertaining. But relax! In this chapter we will look at basic hospitality etiquette including extending and receiving invitations, how to be a courteous host or guest, house guest how-to, and gift-giving guidelines so you'll be covered on many occasions. When you bring your manners to the party, you'll always be on the A-list.

INVITATIONS

Hosts extend invitations to events in many formats: printed card, letter, note, telephone call, email, text, or by online notification. Guests respond by following the reply instructions that accompany the invitation: response card, telephone number, email address, text, online, or in-person response. Simple process, right? Yes, unless a host or guest has a manners meltdown and makes one or more of the classic mistakes associated with invitations.

EXTENDING AN INVITATION

The first impression of your event begins when your invitation lands in the hands or inbox of your guests. You want to make certain that the invitation conveys your vision for the gathering, piques the interest of your guests, and provides a preview of what's to come. Get it right, and your invitation will be your agent of good will, indicating that you are a courteous and gracious host.

When Check with others in your family or circle of friends before choosing your date. You don't want to compete with another event that will draw from the same guest list. Invite guests in a timely fashion. Don't send invitations without sufficient time for guests to reply and make plans to attend. Consider sending a save-the-date announcement to get the word out early.

Who You will be building your guest list in the initial stages of planning your event when not all details have been set. Develop it in two parts—A list and B list—in order to prioritize guests. Once your budget and venue are determined and you know how many people you can accommodate, you'll know if you can include guests from the B list. Never get angry or hold a grudge against someone who declines your invitation. Any number of reasons could dictate their decision.

What Remember to include all pertinent event details: host's name, the occasion, date, time, location, type of event, and a method to respond. Provide a preprinted card, telephone number, or email address and if you want all guests to respond ("RSVP"), or only those who will be unable to attend ("Regrets only"). Optional information that you might include: suggested attire, directions, parking details, and the end time for the event. To keep your invitation text clean and crisp, print some of the add-on information on an enclosure card or direct guests to a party website. Ask several people to proofread your invitation before printing.

How Invitations can be printed—on your computer or by a print shop—or can be extended by email, by telephone, or in person. Planning to use an online invitation? Remember that not all your guests may be computer savvy. You may need to invite some with a phone call.

Why Me? One of the worst jobs a host has to take on is following up with guests who don't respond—it will happen! *Politely* call the guilty parties to inquire and say that you want to confirm that they received the invitation. Let them know how much you hope they can attend and be part of the gathering. A negative attitude in this context can damage relationships. Give the offenders the benefit of the doubt.

ONLINE INVITATIONS

What a great invention—online invitations! They're creative, inexpensive, efficient, and *informal*, the key word in this formula. Think twice about using them for weddings or other formal occasions, and take care that your target audience will be receptive to this form of communication.

Online invitation sources offer hosts template designs, editable fields for text, proofing assistance, a scheduler for distribution and follow-ups, response tracking, and a mechanism for uploading mailing lists. When you want something more traditional than an email in a guest's inbox, most sites offer an option for printed invitations and envelopes which they, or you, can address. Words of warning for hosts using online invitations:

- *Proofread!* And ask someone else to look at your text to back you up.

- Think twice before making the entire guest list and responses public.

- Keep the guest comments field private.

The benefits your guests get from online invitations include handy delivery to their computer, laptop, or smartphone; a one-step response process; a mechanism for including a personal note; and easy access to event details upon receipt and for future reference. Their job? Click on Yes or No. Simple, yet so many invited guests fail to follow through. And what's with the Maybe option? Maybe is a license to be rude and is often used by guests who are waiting for a better offer. A gentle word of advice to these guests: *commit!* If you need to change your response later, do so but not at the last minute. Stay out of the Maybe category, or maybe you won't be invited again.

RECEIVING AN INVITATION

Your invitation really *was* in the mail, and it just landed in your hands or inbox. Woohoo! Now what? Avoid some of the following mistakes, and you'll be branded as a courteous guest and invited again.

Respond, PDQ Always respond to an invitation by the deadline and by the reply method requested (response card, email, telephone call, or online). Remember to indicate your dietary restrictions (not preferences!) or other special needs when you respond, or call the host to report this information. Inform your host if your name is misspelled on the invitation. If you report the error right away, other printed pieces for the event that include your name will be correct, and you will save your host embarrassment later.

R U RUDE? Invitation Etiquette

There can't be an event without an invitation, whether it is extended on engraved stationery or over the phone. So why does a process that should be so basic get so complicated? Because hosts and guests forget some of the common courtesies of giving and receiving invitations.

R U RUDE?	CORRECTIVE MEASURES
You don't have a 100 percent average in responding to invitations.	RUDE on steroids. Failing to respond to an invitation is at the top of the list of annoyances for hosts. You *must* respond to an invitation, and best practice is to do so soon after receiving it. An exception to this rule is when you receive an invitation that includes the phrase "Regrets only" and you are planning to attend.
You are thinking of editing your guest list after a save-the-date announcement has been mailed.	RUDE and (should be) unthinkable. Everyone who receives a save the date *must* be invited to the event or relationships will be damaged. Make decisions about your budget, venue, and anything else that impacts your guest count *before* mailing a save the date. There are no do overs once they are in the mail.
You don't want or expect gifts as part of your event (bravo), so you decide to print "No gifts, please" in the text of your invitation.	Not RUDE, but unnecessary. Standard practice is to omit any mention of gifts on an invitation. When "no gifts, please" is included, it indicates that they are in the scope of the host's thinking, which is what should be avoided. Some guests may call to inquire about gifts, or they will bring one or won't—their choice. Gifts received at the event should be put aside so that non-gifters are not uncomfortable. Write thank-you notes for gifts received.

R U RUDE?	CORRECTIVE MEASURES
You want to bring your girlfriend to the party, but plus-one information is missing from the invitation. The host knows her, so it's OK to include her name when responding.	RUDE and awkward. If the host didn't include your girlfriend's name or "and Guest" on your invitation, she is not invited. It might have been a mistake, or the host decided to invite only the near and dear. Don't call the host to ask if you may bring her nor show up with her in tow. Both would be rude on your part, and you will embarrass her, yourself, and your host.
You are planning a birthday party for yourself at your favorite restaurant. You want to let your guests know how much their meal will cost and figure out how to collect their money.	RUDE times two. You don't collect their money, because it is not appropriate for a host to ask guests to help fund an event. (A few exceptions to this rule might include a group-sponsored gathering, reunion, bridal shower, bachelorette or bachelor party, or a charity event.) If you can't afford to pay for dinner for all of your guests, scale back and plan a gathering that you can afford. And why are you giving a birthday party for yourself? Instead, plan a gathering that will take place around the time of your birthday but don't advertise it as a *birthday party*. Then, toast your guests during the party and say that you gave yourself the present of their company because your birthday was last week. (Better if the date has passed so that guests won't feel the need to rush out and get you a gift.)
You want to include "Regrets only" on your invitation, because you think it will cut down on the number of calls you will have to make and receive.	Not RUDE, just confusing. At first glance, "Regrets only" sounds like a good idea, and then confusion ensues. Some guests will understand that it means they don't have to respond if they are planning to attend. Other guests who are planning to attend will have questions about attire, plus ones, or gifts and will call or email anyway. If your event requires an accurate guest count or you are planning by-name seating, you'll start to doubt the results that "Regrets only" produces, and you'll start calling people to confirm their attendance. Better to go with RSVP and a mechanism for all guests to do so. But, if your event is small and you are blessed with family and friends who are reliable and socially savvy, "Regrets only" might work for your event.

Adults-Only Party

Planning a no-kids gathering? You may mention adults-only in the text of your invitation or in an insert that accompanies the invitation. When using online invitations, include the information in the guest field. In previous ages of enlightenment, people knew the rules of social engagement so a host could convey his or her wishes for an adults-only gathering merely by addressing the invitation envelope to Mr. and Mrs. John Smith. But today, guests feel no shame in asking a host if they may bring their children, a great-aunt, or even a pet. Worse yet, they don't ask at all and show up at the event with these plus ones, twos, threes, or four-leggeds in tow. Don't be that person.

Who's Invited? Never ask if you may bring a guest or children when the invitation is addressed to you alone. Worse, never write in a plus-one name on the response card if the invitation does not indicate that you are invited with a guest. Don't ask to be invited to an event when you haven't received an invitation.

Change of Plans and Can't Attend? After you have responded, you must notify the host immediately if your plans change. Call the host or, if there is enough lead time, write a note to change your yes to a no. Legitimate reasons for changing a yes to a no are illness, family emergency, unexpected out-of-town travel, or a business obligation. Receiving a better offer is *not* an acceptable excuse. If you want to change a no to a yes, call the host to discuss.

But What About . . . ? Always call the host if you have questions. Don't make assumptions about attire, gifts, or other event arrangements.

PARTY PLAYBOOK

Creating a memorable party or event takes more than lining up a venue and planning the perfect menu. It's about gathering congenial people, keeping them engaged in activities and conversation, and making them feel welcome and comfortable. Guests, too, have responsibilities for making an event successful, more than just showing up.

Below are basic job descriptions for party hosts and guests. Study them to improve your job performance.

PARTY HOST HOW-TO

Build the Guest List

Determine what type of party you are hosting—social, business, fundraising, political, product launch?—and build your guest list accordingly. Your best friends need not be invited to every gathering in your home. Think of guest demographics—age, gender, dietary restrictions, physical challenges, politics—when planning your event. Build your party plan with this information in mind.

Have a Game Plan

Create a timeline for preparty chores and the during-party what and when. Provide a comfortable and safe party environment: designated parking, sidewalks and porches cleared and sanded, drop area for coats and belongings, greeter at the door, dry and obstacle-free floors, delineated food and beverage areas, and doors closed to nonparty areas.

Pay attention to the lowly restroom, the step-child of party spaces but important just the same. Provide paper products, hand towels (disposable for large parties), liquid soap, hand sanitizer, air freshener, a trash can, and a plunger tucked into the corner.

Where will guests be permitted to smoke? Someone will ask.

Have a plan for seating guests, for both informal parties and at a dining table. A polite guest will wait for instructions from the host before sitting. Creating a seating plan will help to avoid awkward guest combinations and provide an opportunity for guests to meet new people. Separating couples at the table helps to achieve a better mix. Consider using place cards even at informal gatherings, or guide guests into specific seats.

OLD SCHOOL VS. NEW SCHOOL
How to Respond

Question Help! I received an invitation without a response card or instructions. How do I respond?

Answer Preprinted response cards are a relatively new member of the invitation family. Past generations of hosts and hostesses never needed them, because they could rely on the protocol of their era and the social graces of their guests to generate immediate responses. Guests put pen to monogrammed stationery, and, in their finest penmanship, composed a reply that mirrored the style and language of the incoming invitation. Your response should do the same:

Mr. and Mrs. John Jones *(your name)*

accept with pleasure

the kind invitation of

Mr. and Mrs. James Gardner

to attend the wedding

of their daughter Julia

and Timothy Adams

on

Saturday, February 14, 2018

(or Saturday, the fourteenth of February

two thousand eighteen)

or

Mr. and Mrs. William Payton *(your name)*

regret that due to out-of-town travel

they will be unable to attend

the wedding of

Julia Payton and Tim Stanton

on Saturday, February 14, 2018

If you received a less formal invitation, send a less formal response handwritten on your personal stationery or on a blank notecard with matching envelope.

What's on the Menu?

Don't overextend yourself on a menu that keeps you in the kitchen for long periods of time at the beginning of or during the party. Plan simple foods that you have made before or can be prepared in advance in order to be able to pay attention to your guests. Think about purchasing prepared food to minimize your workload. Quiz guests about their dietary restrictions during the invitation process. It's smart to try to cover all bases with at least one dish that can satisfy each guest on any special diet: vegan, vegetarian, gluten-free, nut-free, dairy-free, alcohol-free, pork-free. If you're a vegetarian, it's OK to plan an all-vegetarian meal for your guests. It's your party. But if you are a carnivore, it is *not* OK to omit vegetarian and vegan options for your guests. For stand-up parties, offer foods that are easy to eat, not messy or challenging. If the menu requires use of a knife, guests must be able to sit down somewhere.

Offer alternatives to alcohol, and monitor alcohol intake. You are responsible for your guests' safety, and you may be liable for underage drinkers or accidents that occur following your event. Assign a family member or friend to bartend to ensure some level of control, or hire a professional server who can tend bar during the party and help with cleanup after.

They're Here!

Be ready on time so that you can greet guests as they arrive. At the beginning of a party, the host or hostess should be at the front door, not the oven door. Designate a pinch hitter to greet if you must be elsewhere. Take coats or show guests where to leave them. Are we taking shoes off today? Where will they be stored? And is it really necessary? It's not a warm welcome, unless a culture-based practice.

Designate a spot where you can place the gifts that some guests may bring. They do not need to be opened during the event. If you receive cut flowers, they should be displayed, so have a vase or two at the ready. (Savvy guests won't bring cut flowers because of the additional work they generate for a host.) If you receive wine or alcohol, you have the option of opening and serving it at the event or putting it aside to use at another time. Make quick notes in a gift log so that you will remember who brought what and can thank them later. Put your phone away as a good example to your guests. Consider officially declaring your party a phone-free zone.

Surprise! Now What?
Learn to handle surprises gracefully—an unexpected guest, a menu item that fails, spills that occur, weather curve balls, the list is endless. Something *will* happen. Always have a plan B in all party categories.

Stir the Guest Mix
Make a conscious effort to introduce guests to one another. Keep a watchful eye on everyone throughout the event, and guide those who may need your help to enter group conversations. Speak to each guest at least once during the party. For large, formal gatherings, consider using a receiving line (see details below) so that you and guest(s) of honor can greet all guests. Split up couples at dining tables.

The Aftermath
Guests will be watching you for cues to know when it's time to leave. Polite signals are standing up from a dining table without an invitation to reconvene in the living room, thanking everyone for coming, asking someone to start bringing out the coats, looking at your watch and stating that you know so-and-so has to get up early the next morning. . . . You'll devise your own plan based on the format of the event and your relationship with your guests. If you're sitting there thinking, "Will these guests ever leave," it's your fault, not theirs.

It is OK to accept offers of help with cleanup, or think about hiring someone for an hour or two after the party ends. If you aren't comfortable having guests clear the table or tidy up your kitchen, thank them and decline the offer. Decide if you want to keep all the leftovers or if you want to distribute them to guests. If you want to give food away, have small disposable containers available for this purpose. Anyone who contributed (not gifted) an alcoholic beverage should leave it with the host, but if you don't want or need it, encourage the guest who brought it to take it home.

If you plan to share photos or post information about the event on social media, check with guests who will be tagged. Do you need to say thank you for a thank-you gift you received? Yes, you owe a note, call, or email to the guests who brought a gift. It's not only the right thing to do, it also lets them know that the gift wasn't lost in the shuffle.

Off-Site Party

If your party will take place in a public venue, you are required to take on the added responsibility of ensuring that the location is:

Accessible Are there physical barriers that would prevent any of your guests from attending? Are there elevators and accessible restrooms?

Accommodating Does the menu offer choices for vegetarians, vegans, and guests who don't consume dairy, nuts, gluten, pork, or alcohol? Is there a lactation room if you know that space will be needed by one or more of your guests? Are there gender-neutral restrooms?

Comfortable Is the venue steering you toward a stand-up reception with no seating so that you can squeeze twenty-five more people in the room? Maybe you need a bigger room *with* seating. And will there be other private parties in the space on the same day that will be competing for resources?

Clean Check for any health code violations. In most cities restaurant inspection results are available online. Take a look at restrooms as a quick way to check the cleaning standards of an establishment.

Safe Consider all aspects of your guests' safety when selecting a venue and planning your event. Are emergency exits adequately labeled, and how are they opened? Are parking lots and sidewalks well lighted and maintained?

Kid-Friendly Even if management assures you that their space is kid-safe, walk around and see for yourself before booking it.

PARTY GUEST GUIDELINES

You were invited to the party because your hosts thought you would (1) make a welcome addition to the guest mix and (2) behave yourself. So, don't leave your manners at home, or your hosts will be sorry they invited you.

Preparty

Dress appropriately. Don't let a wardrobe malfunction be a distraction for you, the host, or other guests. Not sure what to wear to an event? Call the host or party planner, ask a fellow guest, or dress one level above your best guess. It is better to be slightly overdressed than underdressed. Guests show respect for the host and the occasion by dressing up.

Arrival

Arrive on time, but never early. A late arrival demonstrates a lack of respect for or the host and the occasion. An early arrival can catch a host off guard. Call the host if you are running late and give your estimated time of arrival. Poor planning on your part is *not* a legitimate excuse for being late.

When parking in a neighborhood, don't block driveways, intersections, or the host's or a neighbor's front walkway at the curb.

Bring a small gift for the host. Label it with a gift tag or note. Don't assume that the gift will be opened during the party or while you are present. Don't bring cut flowers that require immediate attention. The host may be too busy to stop, find a vase and trim and arrange the flowers. If you bring wine or liquor, don't assume that it will be consumed at the party unless you were asked to bring it as your contribution. Your host may not have been anticipating your gift and has other beverages planned. Suggest that the beer/wine/bourbon gift will be a good accompaniment the next time the host has burgers/fish/cigars, etc.

Party Protocol

Turn off your cell phone before you enter the front door. Try to find and greet the host shortly after you arrive. Always circulate and meet new people. Improve your people skills by giving yourself a meet-and-greet game plan for every event you attend. Yours might be to introduce yourself to at least three (ten, twenty . . . you decide) new people. If you are shy, having such a goal will give you structure for your networking. It's rude—and lazy—to spend time only with people you know. Be enthusiastic. Participate. No phone for the duration. Be in the moment. We have all had a time in our private or professional lives when we were required to attend an event, and we didn't want to be there. Deal with it. Put a smile on your face and make the most of it. You might surprise yourself and have a good time or meet an interesting new person.

Sit down only when invited to do so. Don't put your feet on furniture unless you are certain that it is acceptable, based on your relationship with your host and the informality of the event.

Don't begin to eat or drink before your host invites you to do so or you see that other guests have begun. Taste all dishes that are served unless you have religious restrictions or health concerns.

Never enter areas of the house other than party areas. A closed door means a room or area is off limits. Ready to light up? Not so fast. Never smoke in someone's home without asking permission to do so.

Throughout the party, offer to help set up, wrangle guests, serve, or clean up. Respect your host's response if he or she declines. Spill something but there are no witnesses? The honor system is sacrosanct, so notify your host immediately and offer to clean up.

Be a good citizen when using a bathroom. Remember to lock the door when you enter, get in and out quickly, and leave the room clean. Wipe up any spills, even water and soap, on countertops and errant sprinkles on the toilet seat (somebody has to say it!). It's a public service to let the host know if paper products are depleted or the plumbing is problematic. And no peeking in the medicine cabinet—it could be booby trapped if your host has a dark sense of humor. Note: Let's talk toilets, specifically using other people's toilets. If the thought of using someone else's bathroom for more than just number one causes you to hyperventilate, relax. Just remember that neatness counts, and think about carrying travel-size potty perfume in your pocket or handbag. (Look it up.)

The Party's Over

Don't stay too long. Ask for the end time of the gathering when discussing your attendance with the host, or ask fellow guests who may know. Observe the body language and activity of the host for cues to time your departure. If the host is nodding off, paying the caterer, or loading the dishwasher, those are obvious signs that it's time to go. It is not a good idea to be the last guest out the door, unless you have stayed to help with cleanup.

Always send a handwritten thank-you note by snail mail to your host. Any exceptions? A few. If the party was informal—drinks on the patio, pizza and a football game—or your group of friends rotates hosting responsibilities on a regular basis, then you may send your thank-you by the method of communication you always use with your group—phone, email, or text.

HOUSEGUEST HANDBOOK

HOST HOW-TO

Before

Discuss and determine specific dates and times for arrival and departure. It's not your guest's fault for staying too long if you don't have this discussion before their arrival. And after they arrive, don't feel pressured into agreeing to an extension of the stay if it will disrupt your schedule or household.

Determine how much time you and your guest will spend together during the visit. Manage expectations on both sides by discussing everyone's schedule and plans for the visit prior to arrival. Is this to be a joined-at-the-hip or a ships-passing-in-the-night kind of visit?

During

Provide some measure of privacy for your guest in their guest room or sleeping quarters. Supply basic amenities: bed, sheets, blankets, pillow, towels, clothes hangers, luggage rack, a few toiletries, paper products, alarm clock, reading lamp, window coverings, and modest food and beverage upon arrival.

Discuss the house rules as soon as your guest arrives. Your discussion should cover meal times, quiet hours, security equipment and concerns, and an off-limits list. Don't be shy about discussing sleeping arrangements for unmarried guests and their public and private displays of affection, if those are issues for you. If your guest is not adhering to the house rules, politely address problems as they develop, not after they fester. A slow burn can lead to a flare of tempers.

After

Did the visit go well? Call or email to say you enjoyed seeing your guest and look forward to their next visit (if you mean it). Didn't go well? Change your telephone number and email address and move to a studio apartment.

GUEST GUIDELINES

Before

Don't assume that you may call a relative or friend and say you're on your way. You need to be invited. Once the invitation has been extended and dates are set, communicate any changes to your travel plans and ask if the revisions are convenient for your host. Ask what you should bring.

Ask about and follow house rules and adapt to the household schedule, especially quiet times. Determine the level of shared time between you and your host during your visit. It's rude to use a host's home like a hotel room with little or no interaction, so have this discussion. Don't assume that transportation during your visit will be provided by your host.

During

Keep your host informed of your whereabouts during the visit. Ask before inviting others to join you in the home for a visit or for overnights.

Bring some food or beverages to share, or offer to go for groceries soon after your arrival. Don't eat or drink your host's supplies without asking first. Don't eat in the guest sleeping quarters without permission.

Clean up after yourself in the kitchen, sleeping quarters, bathroom, and other living areas.

Clean means more than making your bed and rinsing out the bathtub. Do you normally leave dirty dishes in the sink, splatters in the microwave, beverage rings on the furniture, mud on the rug, makeup on towels, hair on the bathroom soap or sink, toothpaste on the mirror, smelly workout clothes on the floor? If so, clean up your act. Management will appreciate your efforts. Always use a reasonable share of hot water for showers or baths.

Be discreet regarding clothing, telephone conversations, and amorous adventures. And no eavesdropping.

Don't assume there is free Wi-Fi, and never use the host family's electronic equipment or other items or supplies without permission.

After

Leave your guest room/sleeping area clean and well organized. Dispose of your trash. Ask your host if you should remove linens from the bed and collect towels. If you moved items or furniture during your stay, put them back where you found them.

After your visit, write a note and/or send a gift to thank your host. An email thank-you is not enough.

GIFTS—GENERAL GUIDELINES

To gift or not to gift? Often that is the question that we ask ourselves when occasions arise and we want to share love, friendship, pride, support, or sympathy. What is appropriate? How much is too much—or too little? The gift of good judgment is what we want for ourselves.

WHY

We give gifts for many reasons: when we are a guest; when we observe a milestone in someone's life; and when we want to say, "I thank you," "I am sorry," "I care about you," "I share your joy," "I want to help," "I am proud of you," or "I sympathize." But gifts are never required, for any reason or occasion, so it's up to you to decide if you want to give. Your motivation should be based on your sentiments and on your relationship to the recipient, not because you think there is a rule that dictates you should give. Determine if a gift is really necessary. On some occasions, a card may be sufficient.

To would-be recipients, shame on you if you think you are entitled to a gift because of a milestone event in your life. You are not. There is no constitutional mandate that states gifts are required on specific occasions. When you do receive a gift, you should react as if it is a delightful surprise and show your gratitude immediately, no matter the gift.

WHAT

When possible, select gifts that are specifically related to a recipient's interests. Spend time, as well as money, to choose something appropriate. But don't stress over gift selection if you don't know a person well. Give a gift card instead, which will ensure that the recipient can choose what they like. Personalize the gift by writing a special note on the greeting card that goes with it.

Gifts don't have to come in wrapped packages. Giving of your time or talent can mean a great deal to the recipient: babysitting, dog walking, photography, household chores, home improvement, yard work, transportation, or administrative support. Each of these can be a welcome gift to a friend or neighbor at one time or another.

WHERE

If you bring a gift to a party, secure a tag to the bag or box. Hosts may receive a number of gifts that they set aside and open after the party. You don't want yours to get lost in the mix, and don't expect that the host will open or use your gift during the party.

Don't bring a gift to a wedding reception. Send it to a residence before or after the wedding, or deliver it in person.

HOW MUCH?

Give within your means. Your gift should reflect what you can afford, not what the recipient can afford when they're giving. If there is a cap on spending in group giving, respect the guidelines. It's embarrassing to others when you don't.

If accepting gifts in business is not permitted by the recipient's company or organization, consider making a charitable donation in his, her, or the company's name.

AFTER

Keep a gift log of incoming and outgoing gifts. You don't want to give someone the same thing twice, and you want to remember who gave you the purple sofa pillow so that you can retrieve it from the closet and display it the next time they visit.

There is nothing wrong with regifting, as long as you follow a few basic rules. The item must be new and in its original packaging. It must be something that you know the recipient will like and appreciate. You must avoid giving the item to a friend of the friend or cousin of the cousin who gave it to you. And, most importantly, don't give it back to the person who gave it to you! Your gift log will help here.

For every gift that you receive, write a thank-you note with a specific reference to the item received and how you plan to use and enjoy it.

PARTY PROTOCOL

Let's look at a few of the tools that keep parties running smoothly. They are protocol products and procedures that help hosts to wrangle, identify, and seat guests efficiently.

RECEIVING LINES

The dictionary tells us that a receiving line is "a group of family members and friends who stand in line at a wedding, funeral, or other formal occasion to greet guests and receive their good wishes or sympathy." In a business context, the group of greeters consists of the host, guest of honor, and other host representatives or special guests, all of whom do the same thing as described above—greet guests.

So why include a receiving line in the event that you are hosting? The primary reason is to make your guests feel welcome and to provide an opportunity for each of them to meet their host and guest(s) of honor, something they might miss if the event was completely free-form.

As a rule, receiving lines are planned for events with fifty or more guests. For functions with fewer than fifty, it is assumed that the host and guest(s) of honor will mingle freely and meet all attendees. For functions with no receiving line, it is critical that the host and guest(s) of honor move efficiently through the crowd so that no one feels slighted. Often this requires the assistance of family members at social events or aides or handlers at business, government, or military events.

Host

The purpose of a receiving line is to give the host and guest(s) of honor the opportunity to meet as many guests as possible. That means that guests must move through the line quickly and efficiently.

Keep the number of people in the receiving line to a minimum. Host and guest(s) of honor are usually sufficient, but add spouses if the event is social. If it is a military or business event, include one or two other representatives from the host organization.

The order of the line is usually: (*Introducer—optional*), **host** (*and spouse—optional*), **guest(s) of honor** (*and spouse[s]—optional*), **second host** or **donor** (*and spouse—optional*). Additions may include: **second-ranking guest** and/or **additional hosts.** Wedding receiving lines have a different cast of characters; please refer to the guidelines in chapter 11.

Place the receiving line strategically so that guests are not waiting outside the main event space and there is a way for those who want to bypass the line to move directly into the party.

It is a good idea to assign a family member or organization representative to the end of the greeters' line to monitor the flow of guests and keep things moving. They can also direct guests to event areas as they leave the line.

Determine the schedule for the line with time enough to give members of the line time to enjoy the event. Provide a table behind the line for items they

Receiving-Line History

Mention a receiving line today and most people immediately fall into two camps: those who picture an elaborate occasion where exalted personages are installed center stage to "receive their guests," and those who recall the last wedding reception they attended where they had to shake hands with twelve people when all they wanted to do was greet the bride and groom.

Historically, a receiving line was, indeed, a regimented exercise to control guest access to VIPs because their status required that they be protected. The VIPs greeted their guests, but often with a nod, not a handshake. Today some receiving lines follow protocol and structure similar to their historic predecessors when they involve royalty, heads of state, celebrities, or military officers, but they are a bit less formal in that there is opportunity for a handshake and dialogue.

Modern hosts may decide to include a receiving line in their event when their goal is to greet *all* guests, and they know that it would be impossible to do so while circulating in a reception. The style of the line can be relaxed if the event is not formal, and it can even be as simple as a host or hostess standing at the door to welcome guests. Every line, from old to new, has had the same purpose, and that is to make guests feel important because they have face time with their host.

may need while they are greeting guests—a beverage, hand wipes or sanitizer, handbags, cell phones, and other personal belongings.

Guest

As you approach the line, determine if there is an introducer. This is a person who stands adjacent to, but not in the receiving line, whose role is to control the timing of guest movement, obtain names, and introduce each guest to the host who is first in the receiving line. In most cases, guests don't shake hands with an introducer.

You may talk with other guests while waiting to approach the receiving line, and you may have food or a beverage while waiting in line. As you near the introducer, put down your glass or plate on a drop table or hand it to a server.

Remove your gloves (or at least the glove from your right hand) before moving through the line. Carry belongings in your left hand.

Give your first and last name to the introducer (without shaking hands) who will introduce you to the host. After that, introduce yourself (first and last name) to every member of the line, even if you think someone knows your name, and shake hands.

Move quickly through the line. Offer a short greeting to each member of the line, such as "Thank you for inviting me" or "It is a pleasure to meet you," or "I enjoyed your speech this afternoon." That's all. A receiving line is not the time or place to make a request or to conduct a long conversation.

Never carry food or beverage with you as you go through the line. It is an accident waiting to happen.

It is not appropriate to present your business card or a gift to a member of a receiving line.

Don't attempt to take a photograph while moving through the line, selfie or otherwise.

Never assume that someone knows your name, even if you see or work with the person on a regular basis.

NAME BADGES

We know. You hate name badges, and you're reluctant to wear yours. Even if it isn't a cheesy *Hello, My Name Is* ___ sticker, you look at badges with disdain. Well, change your mind-set and embrace one of the hardest working and most effective tools in your networking toolkit. Never skip an opportunity to wear your badge proudly.

Name Badge Bylaws

Follow these bylaws for maximum badge benefit. When you do your job, your name badge can do its job, and that is to serve as your ambassador.

Do

Wear a name badge high and on your *right* side so that people can glance at your name easily as you shake hands.

When offered a do-it-yourself name badge, print your first and last name and your organization (if it doesn't make your name too small) if in a networking or business context. Never use an honorific for yourself (Mr., Miss, Mrs., Dr.). If the host provides preprinted badges and your name is misspelled or your ID is incorrect, it is better to handwrite the information correctly on a blank badge than to wear the one with the mistake.

Look at a name badge when shaking hands and again at any time in conversation. It's not offensive, it's flattering. And it will help you to follow the Rule of Three, mentioned in the "Name Game" section of chapter 2: say a person's name as you meet, once during your conversation, and again as you part.

Don't

Don't skip the registration table as you enter an event, because you may go through an entire event without a name badge. Not a smart networking move.

If badges are do-it-yourself, don't write too much information on yours so that lettering is small and difficult to read. First and last name are all that matter at most gatherings.

If you're given a name badge on a lanyard or string, tie a knot in the string to raise the level of the badge.

ESCORT CARDS

Escort cards, also known as take-in or seating cards, have one purpose in their short lives, and that is to direct guests to their dining tables at an event with arranged seating. Card styles vary, from a traditional white or ecru miniature envelope with matching card inside to fun and festive tent cards; designer tags; or beribboned event-themed, three-dimensional objects. Fun! ("I see you're holding a starfish. I'm at the same table!") Check party or wedding supply stores or websites for an extraordinary array of creative objects and designs.

Do

Write guests' names on the outside of the miniature envelope and their table number on the inside card. Some cards are preprinted and only need a numeral added to a blank space provided, while others are blank and require the addition of "Table 1." Appoint someone with good penmanship to write on the envelope and inside card, or hire a calligrapher when the budget permits. Use the honorific and last name of each guest.

A best practice is to prepare a card for each individual guest, but some hosts prefer to include a couple or family on one card when they are likely to arrive at the same time and are seated at the same table. Arrange cards, alphabetically by last name, on a table in the reception area. This table can be self-serve or staffed.

It's awkward when your name is misspelled on your escort card. If you spot this early in the reception, inform the host or party planner. There may be time to correct your place card before you arrive at the table. If you pick up the card just before moving to your table, there is nothing you can do at that point. If the event is in a business context, politely notify the host organization after the event so that they can correct their records.

If you notice that there are cards for other guests with your same last name, carefully pick up the one meant for you. To avoid confusion, savvy hosts include the first-name initial for guests with the same last name—"Mr. J. Smith" and "Mr. W. Smith." If you have a question about your card, ask the party planner or a host representative for help.

Don't

When picking up your card, don't pick up cards for other guests with the intent that you will distribute them. Thoughtful, but as you move through a crowded room and stop for conversation, you may forget to hand them off or the guests may get to the table of escort cards before you get to them. Also, often a party planner decides when to invite guests to sit down at their tables based on the status of the distribution of the cards.

Don't misplace your card during the reception or you will have to double back to the table to ask for your seating assignment.

Don't trade cards with other guests so that you can sit at another table. By-name place cards may be at your assigned table, and the seating system will be in chaos if you break rank.

PLACE CARDS

An event host uses place cards for by-name seating for a number of reasons, some of which are to

- scramble guests from various groups and provide more opportunities for guests to meet new people;
- place certain individuals strategically;
- seat VIPs in safe seats for security reasons;
- address guests' disabilities or other special needs;
- reserve a head table for the host and program speakers; or
- separate guests who are at war with one another.

There are various styles of place cards:

- Tent cards that are preset on dining tables at each seat when by-name seating is decreed by the host. Savvy hosts write a guest's name on both sides of tent cards.

- Flat place cards that are placed on dining tables at each place setting. If they are set in the center of a charger or service plate, they are moved by each diner to a spot above the place setting. They need not be propped up for display.

- Tent cards that serve a dual purpose as escort/take-in cards and place cards. They are arranged on a reception table, include the guest's name and a table number, are carried by each guest to the assigned table, and are set above a place setting. Since most guests know their own name at the beginning of an event, it is to the benefit of other guests to turn their name to face the center of the table as a method of introducing themselves to others.

- Name placards for meeting participants, especially those seated at a head table.

CHAPTER 9

MANNERS GO TO WORK

What's the point of learning traditional rules of etiquette in today's high-speed, high-tech world of business? Do you really need to spend time thinking about how to shake hands and greet others, exchange business cards, converse on a number of topics, and dine with dignity? The answer is *yes*, if you care about presenting a professional image, building successful relationships, and earning the respect of your colleagues and clients. People have choices in the business arena, and they choose to do business with people they like and respect.

By learning and exhibiting soft skills, you can develop a demeanor that will increase your level of confidence and comfort in social and business settings. And the key to developing your soft skills is *etiquette*, the rules and traditions of extending courtesy to others. Why not install etiquette in your foundation as you build a more polished you?

JOB INTERVIEW ETIQUETTE

Interview—one of the most fearsome words in the English language for job seekers young and old. Do your hands tremble when you hear the word? You're not alone. Could there be a more difficult situation than walking into a room of strangers, feeling like a suspect under interrogation, knowing your every word and gesture are being evaluated, all while attempting to appear to be confident and professional? As you head out the door for that next important interview, don't forget to pack one of the most powerful business tools available: *etiquette*. Your manners can make the difference between an adequate performance and one that will launch you to the next stage of the hiring process. Your attitude and demeanor are as important as your résumé and experience.

Too many job candidates spend more time worrying about the margins on their résumé than their manners. They fail to realize that employers are selecting individuals not only who have job-related experience but also whom they believe will be a good fit in their business family. They are looking for the human qualities that make the difference in business relationships: courtesy, integrity, and reliability. Manners and respect are the underlying foundation of good relationships, and good relationships are good business.

How do your manners measure up? Use the following information to make certain that they meet the grade.

MAKE AN ENTRANCE

Psychology tells us that we have five to ten seconds to make a first impression. In a job interview, you're given a bit more time to shine—approximately thirty seconds. Since there's no second chance to make a first impression, don't blow this opportunity to cement the image you want to create in the minds of each and every member of an interview team.

You are on stage from the moment you walk into the building where the interview will take place. Smile. Be enthusiastic. Turn off your cell phone before you enter the building. You may be riding on the elevator with the head of your interview team. When you arrive at the office where the interview will take place (never more than ten minutes early), politely introduce yourself to the receptionist (a business card is useful here), and sit at attention in the waiting area—no cell phone or magazines. Stand and shake hands with the person who comes to escort you into the interview.

Enter the interview room with energy and enthusiasm, both of which can help to mask nervousness. Smile, make eye contact, and try to maintain an open posture (align your shoulders with the shoulders of the person you are meeting) as you shake hands with each individual in the room. If possible, walk around the side of the table or desk to shake hands. As you shake hands, introduce yourself using your first and last name, at least to the first person of an interview team. Shake hands with other team members, but it is not necessary to repeat your name each time you do.

WARDROBE MALFUNCTIONS

Always dress up and dress conservatively for a job interview. Even if you are applying for a job behind a steam table in a fast-food restaurant or in the relaxed environment of an IT startup, this is a strategy that works. Remember how your parents told you to dress up to go to church or visit Grandma? Their reasoning was that we demonstrate respect by dressing up. Your polish indicates that you think the interview and potential employer matter, and that you respect them and the interview process.

BODY LANGUAGE SPEAKS BEFORE YOU DO

Employers interpret your attitude and interest in the job and in their company through your body language, just as they do from your answers to their questions. Sit up straight and plant your feet firmly on the floor during an interview. You may think that a relaxed pose will show confidence, but instead it shows a lack of respect or interest. Don't sit with both hands in your lap—you will look like a nervous child. Rest one forearm on the arm of your chair or on the table.

Make eye contact and maintain an open posture, which means aligning your shoulders with the shoulders of the person to whom you are speaking whenever possible. Do the best you can with this when there are a number of people on an interview panel. Do not fidget in your chair, cross your legs, or wring your hands, and try not to use too many hand gestures. Hold a pencil or a pen if that helps to control your nervousness.

WHAT'S IN A NAME?

People love to hear the sound of their name, so use names when you meet interviewers and when you say goodbye. It is not necessary to sprinkle their names throughout the interview. "That's an interesting question, Mr. Davis," will seem artificial if said more than once. Because you may be nervous when entering an interview room, you may not hear and remember all the names of the people you are meeting. To prepare for this, when you are contacted to schedule the interview, ask for the names and titles of the individuals who will be interviewing you. Write them down in the notebook or portfolio that you will carry to the interview, and memorize this list. Then, when you enter the interview room, you can use an individual's name when you shake hands: "Good morning, Mr. Peterson. It's a pleasure to meet you." And always—*always!*—use an honorific (Mr., Ms., Mrs., Dr., General) and last name when meeting someone for the first time in business. When introducing yourself, either in person or on the telephone, use your first and last name without an honorific.

TABLE TALK

After you shake hands with all of your interviewers, stand behind a chair until you are invited to sit down, or politely ask where the interviewer would like you to sit. When you take your seat, do not place personal items on the table—no cell phones, handbags, briefcases, water bottles, or coffee cups. (In fact, never bring a beverage into a job interview.) All of your other possessions should be placed under your chair or on a chair beside you. You may place a portfolio or notepad and pen in front of you. If a beverage is offered, decline politely. Remember to sit up straight with both feet planted on the floor. (See "Body Language" above and on page 23.)

FOR WHOM THE RING TONES

If, for some unfathomable reason, your cell phone rings during an interview, some serious damage control will be required. Do not look at the display to see who is calling, and do not answer it to explain that you cannot talk at that moment. Reach down (because your phone is in your bag under your chair) and hit the off button immediately. Look at the interviewers and say sincerely. "I'm so sorry. I was so caught up in preparing for my interview that I forgot to turn it off." PS If it does happen, you will have to be one of the top candidates in order for the faux pas not to knock you out of the running.

EXIT STRATEGY

When the interview is over, reiterate your interest in the position (if sincere), and thank the group for spending time with you. You may ask about the time frame for filling the job and notifying candidates. Make eye contact, shake hands with everyone in the room, and try to use the name of each individual as you say goodbye. If possible, stop in the outer office to thank the individual who greeted you when you arrived or who escorted you into the interview room. This is not a strategy—just good manners. Keep a smile on your face and your cell phone turned off until you leave the building.

POSTGAME PLAY

Handwrite and snail mail a thank-you note to each person on the interview panel within twenty-four to forty-eight hours of the interview. You will have collected names and titles when the HR or company representative called to set up the interview, or, failing this, you may ask the receptionist for this information as you leave. You may contact the HR representative or the lead interviewer for a status update on the hiring process once the prescribed period of time has passed. You may send interviewers a quick email thank-you message if you believe that your notes will be delayed on your end or theirs, but a handwritten note shows your good manners.

Don't attempt to connect with interviewers on social media. It's not appropriate at this stage.

Notify references of your job search.

Don't underestimate the power of etiquette and people skills in an interview. When interviewers like you, they begin to pull for you to do well, often without knowing they are doing so. Some interviewers will explain questions more fully, help you along when you are searching for a word or an example, and they become more relaxed in how they pose questions and rate your answers. All of these things can help you to succeed in the interview. This emphasis on manners is not intended to diminish the importance of a strong résumé and solid work experience, but to underline how people skills can give one candidate an edge over another.

YOU'RE HIRED! WELCOME ABOARD

Starting a new job is like walking into the middle of a movie. Everyone around you knows what's going on, but you don't have a clue. You wonder if things will ever make sense as you attempt to piece together the plot, identify characters and their motives and relationships, and study the settings for relevant information. As a new hire, you experience many of these same feelings while you sort through the who, what, when, and why of your new work environment. If you want this experience to feel less like you walked into *Titanic* and more like *The Love Boat*, use your manners to guide you and there will be smooth sailing ahead.

Organizations hire a person not only for his or her experience and expertise but also because they believe that the candidate will be a good addition to their business family. In other words, they think they can live with the individual in a business environment day after day. To be the person who quickly blends into the crew of your new professional home, instead of the one who is adrift, follow some basic office etiquette rules and your employers won't be sorry they brought you on board.

DRESS CODE

You dressed up and conservatively for your job interview, no matter the industry or position, but when you report to work you want to be on the same page with your coworkers. Ask a human resources representative or your new supervisor for dress code guidance. As a rookie, never dress to the lowest level of what the code permits, even on casual Fridays. Instead, as people are forming their opinions about you, dress to the highest level of the standard recognized in your workplace. This gesture shows that you are professional, are serious about your work, and respect your employer.

SMILE

So basic, but means so much. You have five to ten seconds to make an impression, so pay close attention not only to the clothes on your back but also to the look on your face. Don't give others the opportunity to label you as unfriendly, haughty, preoccupied, spaced out, or any other misinterpretation because of what they read on your face. You'll be amazed at the effect that your smile has on others. It says that you are a confident, approachable, and likeable individual. PS Wear a smile like a mask, if necessary, to hide that you are nervous or uncomfortable.

INTRODUCE YOURSELF

Remember that 85 percent of your success in business is based on your people skills, so extend your hand and say your first and last name to everyone who crosses your path. And, while doing so, stand up straight, make eye contact, and always smile. You may not remember the names of all the people you meet the first week on the job, but they will remember you as being friendly, outgoing, and confident.

TAKE NOTES

It is impossible to remember everything that comes your way during the first weeks on the job, but if you take notes after you meet coworkers, obtain information, or receive assignments, you'll feel more confident and in control. And the more quickly you remember names, the sooner you'll fit in.

LAY OF THE LAND

Don't jump into things with both feet. Instead, proceed with caution as you survey your new territory for temperature and conditions. How formal or informal is the business environment? What is the chain of command? How strict is management on various issues? Remember, you are being watched and evaluated, so follow the rules. If your supervisor says lunch breaks are forty-five minutes and your coworkers tell you that they take an hour and no one cares, be back at your desk in forty-five minutes.

SHARED AREAS

Unless you'll be working from home all day, every day, you'll be spending some of your time at work in common areas shared by all staff. These areas include conference rooms, libraries, document-preparation space, pantries, break rooms, and restrooms. Be a good citizen and do your part to maintain these areas.

KNOCK BEFORE ENTERING

When you enter a cubicle, office, or conference room that is occupied, knock. Ask the occupant if it is a convenient time to ask a question, share some information, or retrieve something from the room. It is extremely rude not to do so. Open work spaces? Your behavior doesn't change with the absence of walls. Imagine a door before interrupting someone at their desk. Wait "outside" until you are invited "in."

CONNECT WITH OTHERS

Make certain that your radar is working as you begin to interact with coworkers, supervisors, and clients. On any given day, you could be working with four generations of people. Each person, and each generation, has a unique style and deals with people in different ways. Some people want only the facts and business-related data. They don't want to be your friend, and they don't want you to waste their time. Others want to hear about your weekend, family, or new apartment before starting a business discussion. Learn to read the signals that others send, and adapt your approach accordingly.

BE A TEAM PLAYER

Your employer hired you because he or she thought you would fit in and be a good addition to the business family. Demonstrate your willingness to be part of that family whenever you can. When extra hours are required on an important project, a coworker needs help, a phone needs coverage, or other special circumstances arise, do your part to help. Show that you are willing to do some extra lifting, even if it isn't in your job description. It's important, too, to participate in some, though not necessarily all, after-hours activities when invited.

CHECKLIST: Personal Fouls

CUBICLE AND DESK VIOLATIONS

* general disorganization and clutter that creeps into adjacent areas

* entering a coworker's space without knocking

* interrupting telephone calls or meetings

* eavesdropping or gossiping

* humming or singing

* loud conversations in person or on the phone

* using speaker phone often

* eating foods with offensive odors

* slurping or chewing loudly

PERSONAL GROOMING AND HYGIENE VIOLATIONS

* taking off shoes

* walking around barefoot

* too much perfume or cologne

* grooming hair or nails

* applying makeup

* flossing or dry brushing teeth

* blowing nose loudly

* sneezing without covering mouth and nose

* failing to use hand sanitizer

If a coworker is guilty of any of these violations and it's affecting your quality of life, have a friendly talk with the offender in a private setting. Do it soon after the problem arises; don't let your annoyance or anger escalate. Suggest solutions to the problem. If you are uncomfortable initiating the discussion, register your complaint with your supervisor. It is his or her responsibility to intervene.

GENDER-NEUTRAL COURTESY

In business, courtesy is gender-neutral. We don't decide if, how, or when to extend courtesy or assistance based on gender. We, men and women, do so for other reasons. Below are some of the occasions and situations where a man or woman can and should step in to help, in a *business context*:

- **Assisting with a Coat** Anyone in the vicinity helps a person who is struggling with a coat or wrap.

- **Paying for a Meal** The host pays for the meal, regardless of gender.

- **Standing** In business, both men and women stand when a superior enters a meeting room, when greeting a client or colleague at a conference table or dining table, and when meeting new people. (In *social* settings, we revert to tradition, and a woman, on most occasions, may remain seated when greeted and when shaking hands.)

- **Helping with a Chair** In a business setting, it is not necessary or appropriate for a man to assist a woman with her chair. However, a man or a woman should step in to assist an individual of either gender who is incapacitated and needs help in any way.

- **Carrying Boxes of Meeting Materials** The host of the meeting does this, with the help of anyone she or he can round up.

- **Entering and Exiting an Elevator** When alone, enter an elevator in the order that you arrived to wait at the elevator bank. To exit, people closest to the door leave first, followed by middle- and back-row passengers. If escorting someone, allow your guest to enter first, and then enter and press the button to select your floor. When you arrive at your floor, exit first, put a hand to the doors to prevent them from closing as your guest exits, and then lead your guest to your destination. Gender is not a factor in elevator protocol in a business context.

Historical Gender Courtesies

For centuries, gentlemen were instructed to extend certain courtesies to women because women were considered the gentler sex and in need of special assistance. Whoa! Not an appropriate mind-set today. Women are professional equals and don't appreciate being pampered for the wrong reason: that others think they are incapable of taking care of themselves. But because these historical courtesies are part of early training for some men, they are instilled in their character and are not easy to switch off and on. In social settings, these men are golden, but in business they need to don gender blinders and be courteous to all.

If and when women are on the receiving end of these historical courtesies in business, they should not feel slighted or offended, but instead accept them graciously, without offense, and without embarrassing male colleagues or clients.

The following courtesies should be reserved for *social* settings:

- Men help a woman with her coat.
- Men assist the woman on their right with her chair at a dining table (and a woman on their left, if no one is assisting her).
- Men stand when a woman leaves a dining table and when she returns. A half-rise from the chair is sufficient in most cases.
- Men open doors for a woman, both in a building or on a car.
- Men enter a revolving door first when it is not moving.
- Men enter a taxi before a woman, move across the seat, and allow the woman to sit in the right rear passenger seat (right-hand traffic). When they reach their destination, men exit the taxi street side and move around the vehicle to open the woman's door.

- Men allow women to precede them when walking in a narrow area or going through a door.
- Men walk on the street or curb side of a sidewalk when accompanying a woman.
- Men hold an umbrella over their female companion, even if it means getting rain soaked themselves.
- A man may offer an arm to a woman for support when walking on uneven ground, steps, or other hazardous areas, but he should not grasp her elbow or arm to steer her in a particular direction.

BUSINESS CARDS—OWNER'S MANUAL

When faced with a dilemma at work, have you ever found yourself wishing that you could reach for operating instructions to help you navigate the challenge? If business-card protocol has ever given you pause, here is an owner's manual that will keep you on the right path.

WHY THEY MATTER

The basic role of a business card is to provide a quick and effective method for identifying yourself and distributing your professional contact information. A closer look reveals the higher purpose they serve: they are an extension of who you are. They are you when you're not there in person to exhibit your professional polish. But many of us have a love-hate relationship with our business cards, because they often raise more questions than they answer. How should they look and feel? What information should be included? How and when are they used? How many should be distributed? What do we do with cards received? Time to turn the spotlight on the protocol of business cards.

MAKE AND MODEL

Your card is a symbol of your brand and should project the image that you want for yourself and your employer. If you work in a field where tradition and a conservative ilk are mainstays of the corporate culture, a conservative card—black lettering printed or engraved on a heavy, white card stock—will help you to present that image. If art, design, or cutting-edge technology is your number-one product, the use of color, graphics, or die-cut shapes may help you get your message across and make a bold and lasting impression. But before allowing your creativity to run wild, remember that the standard size for business cards in most North American, Latin American, and European business communities is 3½" × 2". When you deviate from this standard, you run the risk that your card will be incompatible with scanning and vCard technology, and that it won't fit into the card wallets, folders, and binders that many people still use to organize cards they receive. Odd-shaped, oversized, or folded cards may attract attention, but they can be a nuisance to manage.

The standard information to include on your card is your name, title, company name, mailing and/or street address, contact numbers (office telephone, cell, and fax), and email address. Many business professionals choose to include their company logo and website address as well.

Consider printing a social card or an alternate business card to present in circumstances when it would be undesirable or inappropriate to give your office contact information. This idea also allows you to explore a more creative look for your secondary card, one that showcases your personality or your interests more than a traditional business card can.

Avoid using DIY cards you print at home, unless you use heavy, high-quality paper and the edges are smooth, not perforated.

CARE AND MAINTENANCE

Business cards have a shelf life. Examine your cards periodically and discard the ones that look tired. Never distribute a card that is soiled, creased, or looks as if it has been hibernating in the bottom of your briefcase.

Keep your card information up to date—no handwritten corrections. If your contact information or title has changed recently and you must use an outdated card while waiting for a reprint, say to the recipient, "My email address has changed. May I give you my new address?" and then write it on your card. This makes it appear as if the change has just occurred. Or you may ask for their card and say that you will send your contact information to them, because your card is being reprinted.

TIPS AND TECHNIQUES

Keep your cards handy. You won't look professional if you have to dig to the bottom of your handbag or briefcase or turn your pockets inside out when you need one. Present your business card with the text facing the recipient. When you show respect for your own card, others will treat it with respect. If you want to stand out in some way when presenting your business card, think about the method as much as the message—extracting your card from a show-stopper card case or saying your name or your company's name in such a way that it will be remembered.

Give your card to a receptionist when you visit an office as a method of introducing yourself. Ask before taking a card from someone's desk during or after a meeting or interview. Place the cards you receive from others separate from your cards so that there are no mix-ups when reaching for your card.

Look at a business card when it is presented to you, thank the presenter, and carefully put the card away. Write pertinent notes on it later, not when the card owner is present.

In most instances, you should allow a superior to initiate the exchange of business cards. When one person clearly outranks another, the junior should not extend a card until the senior has done so. Also, the junior should not ask the senior for a business card but should wait until it is offered.

Connect with someone before presenting a card or asking for a card. In most cases, it is not the first thing you do when meeting others, but stop, look, and listen to what is happening around you. In some industries, the exchange is at the beginning of a meeting with many people participating. When this happens and you have collected several cards, it is smart to arrange them in front of you on the conference table in the order that people are seated, and refer to them during the meeting for names, titles, and responsibilities. Follow up on business contacts shortly after meeting someone and exchanging cards. If you promised to send information, do so in a timely fashion. Delivering on your promises is part of your brand.

Don't present a business card at a social function, unless it is the only method of conveying your contact information when it is requested. You may want to have a social card printed to use in nonbusiness-related functions. Never present a business card in a receiving line.

PRODUCT WARNING

What is the difference between a business card and an advertising flyer? If you don't know, please continue reading. The primary purpose of a business card is to present your contact information, ideally after you have made a connection with the recipient. A business card is not an overt advertisement for you or your business and is not distributed in the manner of a flyer. Steer clear of promotional gimmicks disguised as business cards. Who came up with the idea of business cards that include a teeny, tiny résumé printed on the back? Don't go there.

Don't confuse yourself with a Texas Hold'em dealer when you attend conferences, receptions, or networking events. It is not your goal to place your card in every outstretched hand within close range. When you do so, you are perceived as someone who is trying too hard and is desperate for contacts or attention.

CHECKLIST: Elevator Etiquette

All elevators have a routine maintenance checklist, and elevator passengers do as well. Read the passenger performance requirements below, and your behavior will always pass inspection.

* Stand to the right when waiting for an elevator to arrive, and allow people to exit before you enter.

* If others have been waiting before you, allow them to enter before you do.

* A man allows a woman to enter an elevator first in *social* situations only. Courtesy in business is gender-neutral.

* Don't try to squeeze into an overcrowded elevator.

* If riding alone, move to the rear. Strangers, go to your corners.

* Always face forward toward the doors.

* Hold belongings low and in front of you.

* Standing close to the buttons? You're the designated driver, so offer to help others.

* Keep conversations to a minimum—nothing confidential, no gossiping, and no cell phones.

* Hold the doors open for others on their way to the elevator.

* Do-si-do with other passengers to allow others to exit, and politely announce your exit if you are moving from the back.

* If you are able, take the stairs when going up or down one or two floors. Your popularity will increase tenfold, as will your stamina.

* **Extra Credit** When escorting a business superior or client, allow them to enter the elevator first. Once you have boarded, press the button to select your floor. Because you were last in, you'll be first out and can lead your colleague to your destination.

MEETINGS MANNERS

It is safe to say that Woody Allen wasn't referring to business meetings when he said, "Eighty percent of success is showing up." A great deal more is required to produce or participate in a successful meeting—planning, preparation, facilitation, active listening, contributing, and follow-up. When stakeholders bring their manners to the table, the proceedings run more smoothly and goals are achieved more quickly.

PARTICIPANT PLAYBOOK

Many busy professionals view meetings as an interruption of their "real" work, and this attitude shows in their demeanor. But, when they change their mind-set about meetings, prepare strategically, and participate as an active stakeholder, their performance in and takeaways from meetings improve dramatically.

Prepare

- Know why you're attending a meeting. Because you were invited is not the answer. What's your role and how should you prepare? Don't waste the time of the host or other participants by just showing up.

- If an agenda is sent in advance of a meeting, read it and think about it.

- Research the dress code of where you're going. Dress appropriately to show respect and look like a serious professional.

Arrive on Time

- In business, if you're not five minutes early to a meeting, you're late.

- If unforeseen circumstances cause you to arrive late, quietly slip in and do not interrupt. If an opportunity presents itself for you to apologize briefly (perhaps as you begin your first contribution to the discussion), do so. At the least, try to make eye contact with the host and silently mouth, "I'm sorry."

- Explain your tardiness to the host at the end of the meeting.

On Your Feet

- Stand behind a chair at the meeting table until you are invited to take a seat. For any number of reasons, a meeting organizer may have planned a specific seating arrangement.

- Introduce yourself to others as they approach their seats. Once you are seated, if others approach to shake hands, stand up.

- Room too warm? Don't be the first person to remove your jacket or sweater. Wait for the meeting host to initiate.

Business Cards

- If cards are exchanged prior to the start of a meeting, arrange them in front of you on the conference table in the order that people are seated.

- Use them for reference throughout the meeting. This will help you to keep names, titles, affiliations, and responsibilities clear in your mind.

- Don't write on the cards during the meeting.

Stuff

- Don't place your personal belongings on the table when you take your seat—no cell phones, briefcases, car keys, sunglasses, or handbags. Place these items under your chair or on an empty chair beside you.

- You may place on the table a portfolio, laptop or tablet (if they are to be used for the meeting), a pad of paper, the meeting agenda, and supporting documents.

Refreshments

- First time meeting with someone, or meeting in a new venue? Don't arrive with a water bottle, coffee cup, or food. If you do, you demonstrate a lack of respect by being too informal too soon.

- If the meeting organizers offer food or beverage, you may accept. However, if you are nervous prior to a presentation or uncomfortable in the new surroundings, skip the amenities and focus on the agenda.

- If food or beverages are offered by the meeting host, never take more than a small portion, unless you want to be branded as a glutton.

Focus

- Turn off electronic devices before entering a meeting room.

- If you forgot to turn off your cell phone and it rings during a meeting, immediately apologize and say, "I am so sorry. I thought I had turned it off." Then, reach down (because you have placed the phone under your chair in your handbag or briefcase) and turn it off *without checking the display and/or answering to say that you will return the call.*

- If you are expecting a *critical* business call during a meeting, explain this to the host prior to the start of the meeting. Place the phone on silent mode, keep it out of sight in your pocket or lap, and quietly excuse yourself from the room when the call comes in.

Listen Up
- Demonstrate active listening techniques (see chapter 2).

- Don't interrupt others when they are speaking, and don't monopolize a discussion. If you have been allotted ten minutes on the agenda, don't speak for fifteen.

- Ask questions when and if you need clarification on topics discussed, especially those related to your takeaway assignments.

- When attending a virtual meeting, sit in a quiet spot, mute the discussion when you are not speaking, and don't multitask.

For the Record
- Take notes. They may help you or others later. The process may help you to stay alert.

- If you are assigned responsibilities, note the specifics of your tasks and your deadlines.

- Don't audio or video record the proceedings, even if only for the purpose of note taking, without clearing it in advance with the meeting host or organizer. If recording is approved, inform meeting participants that you are doing so.

It's Not Over 'til It's Over
- Stay to the end of the meeting unless you have informed the host in advance that you must leave early.

- If business cards were not exchanged at the beginning of the meeting, introduce yourself to the people you will be working with and give your card and ask for others' cards after the meeting adjourns.

- Don't overlook networking opportunities at the end of a meeting.

Leave No Trace
- Remove all items you brought into a meeting room.

- Offer to assist the meeting host to clear away meeting materials and trash.

HOST HANDBOOK

Get Ready

- Determine why you are scheduling the meeting. Because it's Tuesday and we always meet on Tuesday is not sufficient reason.
- Prepare and distribute an agenda prior to the meeting. This sets the tone for an organized, no-nonsense meeting, and it indicates that you respect the participants and their time.
- Test technology and equipment in advance of the meeting.

Get Set

- Arrive early in order to set up the room, retest equipment, distribute handouts, and greet and seat participants.
- Have a strategic seating plan in mind, and guide participants into the right seats.
- Make certain that the temperature of the room is comfortable. Too warm? Be the first to take off your sweater or jacket to indicate that others may do so. Comfortable participants are more attentive and productive.
- If you are offering food and beverage, confirm that it is ready, is accessible, and includes healthy options. Invite participants to serve themselves as they arrive. Refreshments can be a distraction, however, so they are not appropriate for all meetings.

Go

- Start the meeting on time. Demonstrate respect for the participants who arrived on time, and set a precedent for punctual meetings.
- Introduce everyone in attendance, including virtual attendees and support personnel who may be there to assist with equipment or note taking. It is rude not to do so. If you do not know everyone in the room, you may say, "Let's introduce ourselves before we begin."
- Ask a participant or a member of your team to serve as meeting facilitator in order to keep to the schedule and agenda. Designate a note-taker and, after the meeting, distribute the notes to all participants. If you plan to record video or audio of the proceedings for any reason, inform participants before the meeting begins.
- Announce your meeting protocol, whatever it may be—cell phones off and out of sight, introduce yourself before speaking, raise hands before speaking, facilitator will time remarks and responses, etc.

- Give a brief overview of the meeting agenda and state the desired outcome.
- For long meetings, schedule a sufficient number of breaks. The first break after lunch should be one hour into the afternoon session.

Stop
- Begin to summarize a few minutes before the end of the meeting. Review assignments and deadlines that have been discussed.
- End on time. Respect participants' schedules. Don't assume that they can remain beyond the end time that was announced. If your meeting runs long, you could delay meetings that may follow yours in the same room.

Wrap Up
- Set dates for follow-up meetings.
- Review notes taken and distribute them to participants, highlighting their assignments and deadlines.
- Establish a system for ensuring that deadlines are met.
- Remove all meeting materials, equipment, and trash from the meeting room.

EZ EMAIL ETIQUETTE

What's not to like about email? It can be quick, informative, efficient, and . . . informal. Ah, there's the problem waiting in the weeds for all who email in business. We are becoming too informal when using this method of communication at work.

In our personal lives, we may go to great lengths to establish a unique email persona by liberally sprinkling our messages with humor, abbreviations, color, creative fonts, and a legion of emojis. But think for a moment about your business environment and network. On any given day, you will interact with three to four generations of people, and only a small percentage of those will LOL at an informal approach to business email.

The number-one reason for adopting a more formal approach for business email is to show good judgment and respect for those with whom you are communicating. When you begin a new business relationship by email, compose your messages as if you were putting the same information on company stationery and sending it by snail mail. Once a relationship is established, you may become more informal as you become adept at mirroring the style of your recipients.

Just as you need two wardrobes, one for your personal and one for your professional life, you need to establish two email images for yourself and to know instinctively where the line is drawn to separate the two. When in doubt, move that needle in your brain to the formal side of the gauge. You will never offend someone by being too formal, but you will offend some individuals by being too informal too early in a relationship.

BEST PRACTICES

Salutation In most instances, you should open email messages with a salutation: "Dear Ms. Smith"; "Good morning"; "Hi, team"; "Happy holidays!" Once an email exchange is established and you are sending quick updates or responses back and forth, a salutation is not always necessary.

Honorific When beginning a business relationship via email, use an honorific (Mr., Ms., Mrs., Dr., General) and last name in the first few messages you exchange with a contact or client. IT SHOWS RESPECT (emphasis here, not shouting) and helps to launch a relationship in a positive way. This rule applies to *all* recipients, even if you know they are your age or younger and no matter what position they hold in their organization. After a few email exchanges, they will begin to address you by your first name or sign their messages using their first name only. These are green lights for you to relax your style and use their first name in your messages. With most contacts, you will begin to use first names after a message or two. With others—some supervisors, senior-level members of your organization, clients—you may never get beyond the honorific.

Subject Line Always write specific information in the subject line, and change it each time the contents of your message changes. People often skip over an email that includes a subject line they have seen before, thinking it is old business. And never write your entire message in the subject line. Most people find it annoying.

Message Contents Write like a reporter. Don't bury your lede. The first sentence and paragraph in your message is your breaking news and tells the recipient why you are emailing. Be concise. Assume your message will be read quickly.

Need to send a long message? Number the items within the message. It organizes your thoughts and the recipient can place comments or answers next to each item. Also, numbering helps to ensure that the recipient won't miss one of your points and send you an incomplete response.

CHECKLIST: Telephone Etiquette

In business, an entire relationship can be conducted over the telephone. Your telephone manners are as important as your face-to-face, one-on-one calls.

* Smile when you answer a call.

* Answer calls professionally. *Hey* is *not* a greeting in business

* Identify yourself when answering.

* Use active listening techniques, focus, and don't multitask.

* Take notes when necessary.

* At the end of a call, summarize the information exchanged.

* Transfer calls carefully, and explain what you are doing. Provide the name and number of the person to whom you are transferring the call.

* Use please and thank you often.

CONFERENCE CALLS

* Know your role in the call.

* Identify yourself when you speak.

* Don't interrupt.

* Practice active listening techniques; don't multitask.

* Control noise in your area, and mute your phone when you are not speaking.

* Be a serious participant. Informality and humor may fall flat when not face-to-face.

* Take notes.

* At the end of the call, confirm your assigned tasks or next steps that involve you or your team.

VOICEMAIL TIPS

* Record a professional greeting.

* Keep your greeting current.

* Check your voicemail box often and manage your messages.

* Try to return calls within one day.

* Leave clear and concise messages.

* Phone tag with no content is *dumb*. Use your voicemail intelligence and leave questions and/or answers in your messages.

Spelling and grammar count. They are part of our brand. Proofread!

Respond when receiving something you requested. A quick "Thanks! Got it" lets the sender know the message didn't land in a spam folder. This is not a waste of time. It's confirmation on both sides and common courtesy.

Don't use your business email to forward gossip, jokes, chain letters, or other non-work-related messages or attachments. Delete these items, without responding, when they appear in your mailbox.

Recipients Double-check the recipient list. Beware of Reply to All. People have been fired for sending confidential information to the wrong recipients.

Respond Always try to respond within twenty-four to forty-eight hours. (That's not a typo.) Even if you do not have an answer to the sender's question or request, send a quick response that says you received the message, and give an estimated time frame for your response.

Manage your expectations for receiving responses. Everyone won't follow your lead of responding quickly, because they may be overwhelmed with email (and not as organized as you) or schedule only one or two times a day to read and respond. Your deadline is not necessarily their deadline. Need something faster? Call, text, or schedule a face-to-face.

Email Privacy? You must be joking! Never assume that anything you email is private, no matter what you say in a subject line, heading, or introductory paragraph There are numerous reasons and ways that your message can go astray. Instead of spending sleepless nights worrying about something you said, write every message as if it will be printed and posted on the company bulletin board. Confidential information should be delivered and discussed by telephone or in face-to-face meetings, not emailed.

Recall a Sent Message? You're out of luck. It is not always possible to recall a message you have sent in error or anger, even when attempting to retract it immediately. The best damage control is to admit your error, apologize if necessary, and learn from your mistake. Don't ever email angry. Instead, compose your message, save it as a draft, and store it overnight. Reread the message the following day, after you have had time to cool off, and edit it accordingly.

Reply to All? Do you really mean *all*? Proceed with caution when you hit Reply to All vs. Reply. You may be sending your message to everyone who has ever been part of the email chain of messages, and you may be including a forgotten someone who was sent a copy of an earlier message.

Group Email When you have developed a group list, large or small, it is courteous not to reveal the email addresses of the entire list to all recipients. Explore the options of your email system that allow you to keep your list confidential.

QUICK TIP
Bottom-Up Email

Adopt the bottom-up approach to email, and you will become more proficient and make fewer errors.

6. **Send.**

5. **Confirm recipients.** Add or subtract?

4. Check the **subject line.** Does it need to be updated?

3. If you mention **attachments,** are they attached?

2. **Proofread** your message.

1. **Compose the message.** Remember, a strong beginning will get your message read, so don't bury your lede. Say why you are writing or ask for what you need in the first sentence. (Or the second sentence, if you begin with a "hope all is well" opening.)

Signing Off Always include your contact information in a signature block. Make it a permanent component of your content field. Don't make a recipient look through old email messages to find your phone number or mailing address.

CHAPTER 10

DINING DECODED

Your dining skills become increasingly important as you enter new social and business arenas. You will be invited to dine with family and friends at milestone celebrations, the parents of your significant other, job interview panel members, and business colleagues and clients. Your goal should be to eat food gracefully and not wear it. On these occasions, your primary focus is on accomplishing the goals of the gathering. You are dining to build relationships. Don't let poor dining skills sabotage your success.

GENERAL GUIDELINES

Master the following general dining etiquette rules, and you'll be comfortable at any table with anyone.

GET READY

Find your seat and stand behind your chair to greet other diners as they join the table. If everyone is already seated when you arrive, sit down and introduce yourself to the diners on your immediate right and left. Try to speak with others at your table during the meal.

Don't place personal belongings on a dining table—no cell phones or other electronics, sunglasses, car keys, handbags, pillboxes, or portfolios, and don't bring a glass to the table from a cocktail reception. When at a working lunch or dinner, don't initiate the agenda (printed or verbal) until after the entrée is served (lunch) or dessert is served (dinner), unless your colleague or client initiates a discussion earlier.

Pull yourself in close to the table so that there is about six to eight inches between the table and your abdomen (the combined width of the palms of your hands). Your food will have a shorter distance to travel to your mouth.

Dining Warm-Up

It's a fact that dining gracefully in stressful situations is hard, so think *soft start* as you begin each new experience:

Slow Down Don't dive into your seat, your place setting, or your food.

Observe Watch your host and other diners for cues. Look at your place setting for clues to what's to come.

Focus Be in the moment. Don't be distracted by your nerves, expectations, cell phone, or agenda.

Think Make strategic choices about where to sit, when and what to order, topics and timing of conversation, speed at which to dine, and how formal or informal to be.

If grace or a blessing is offered, sit quietly and respectfully.

Don't be the first man to remove your suit coat or jacket. Wait for the host to take the lead. If there is no host, follow the lead of others, but always begin with formality.

In most instances, it is polite to wait for your host or hostess to take a napkin from the tabletop, a sip of a beverage, or a bite to begin a course. In business dining there may not always be a host at your table or the host doesn't know to take the lead. Observe and use your judgment. If no one is leading, place your napkin in your lap shortly after introducing yourself to fellow diners and before touching anything else on your place setting.

When dining in a private home, don't begin to eat until everyone at the table has been served and your host begins. At weddings, charity events, and banquets where tables are set for eight or more guests and don't include a host, it is not necessary to wait for all guests to be served before beginning to eat. Service is often irregular and food for an entire table doesn't always arrive at once. You may start when others seated near you are served (your minicommunity). If others have been served and you have not, encourage them to begin.

If you are a fast eater, slow down; if you are a slow eater, speed up. Try to pace yourself with other diners around you, especially when dining in business. If you notice that others have finished and you have not, end quickly so that the course can be cleared.

GET SET

Look at your place setting for a preview of what's to come. Don't rearrange your place setting; use pieces where they are set. This may require some reaching toward your bread plate and various glasses, but you are up to the challenge. Just mind your shirtsleeves. Glasses may be shifted slightly, in order to bring your water glass forward if you are not drinking wine.

Once a utensil has been used, it must never go back on the table, tablecloth, or placemat. Place it on a plate or saucer.

Place trash that you generate—sugar packets, plastic butter containers, straws, stirrers—on the edge of a plate, not on the table, tablecloth, or placemat. Fruit slices that accompany some beverages should be dropped into the beverage or placed on the side of a plate.

Drop something? Don't dive under the table to retrieve a napkin or utensil. Ask your server or host for another.

GO

Food is served from the left and removed from the right side of each diner. Beverages are served and removed from the right. You may need to shift occasionally to make room for a server to place your items.

Don't feel pressured to drink alcohol or eat anything that you normally choose not to eat because of your religion, health, or habit. However, in order not to offend your host, you should taste dishes that have been prepared especially for the occasion if they do not conflict with your restrictions. Prior to international travel, research customs and traditions to learn where and when you *must* accept food and beverages that are offered.

You don't have to finish all the food on your plate. If you are served something that you don't like, ignore it, but don't complain about it.

Never speak with food in your mouth, chew with your mouth open, or lick your lips.

Eat and drink in moderation. In most cultures, no one is offended if you leave food on your plate, but you are offensive in every culture if you overeat or drink too much.

When dining for business, don't offer your food to others or ask to sample a companion's food.

STOP

When you have finished a course or your meal, don't push plates away from you or stack dishes.

Personal hygiene is never conducted at a dining table. Go to the restroom to reapply makeup or to clean your teeth or hands.

In restaurant dining, remember to tip your server according to service, not food quality or preparation. That is the responsibility of management.

Don't take leftovers away from a lunch or dinner unless dining with family or close friends.

PASSING FOOD

You may reach forward for items that are directly in front of you. Don't reach to the left or right beyond your place setting. Ask your table companions to pass what you need.

Food is passed to the right . . . except when it's not. Exceptions to the rule include a second pass of an item when diners should use common sense and pass the shortest distance required to reach the diner who requested the item.

Pass the following items immediately after a corresponding course has been served: bread, butter, salad dressing, sauces, and gravy.

Items that need not be passed until someone asks for them include: condiments, lemon slices, sugar and cream, and salt and pepper (which are passed together always).

On the initial pass of an item:

- The diner who can reach directly in front of his or her place setting is responsible for getting an item started around the table.
- Pick up the item to be passed—bread basket, sauce or salad dressing, butter dish—and, while holding it firmly, offer it to the diner on your left with a cordial, "Would you like some bread before I pass it?"
- That diner takes a piece, you take a piece, and then you pass the basket to your right.
- The last person receiving the basket places it on the table in front of their place setting.
- At a large dining table, there may be multiple serving pieces of the same item placed at intervals. This passing pas de deux will happen at several locations on the table.

Completing a Pass

Did you hear the one about the table of eight adults who finished two full courses at dinner without bread, butter, or salad dressing because everyone at the table was too timid to initiate the passing of these items or to ask someone else to do so? No punchline here; just the sad image of people who wanted bread but were too unsure of their dining skills to reach for a roll. This will never happen at your table if you take the lead and pass like a pro. All you need to do is focus on these four important points:

1. No foul for reaching directly forward to pick up items in front of you on the table.

2. Passing is to the right, except . . .

3. on the initial pass of an item when it is offered first to the diner on the initiator's left, taken by the initiator, and then passed to the right.

4. If you are not in position to initiate a pass, ask the diner who is nearest the item to do their job.

If no one takes the lead on passing an item, look directly at the person who is closest to the item and politely ask them to do so. For this initial pass, diners may take the item as it comes to them and continue to pass it to the right. Don't shortstop the food while it is on a subsequent pass. It is impolite to serve yourself before the item reaches the diner who made the request for seconds. Once that requesting diner has taken the item, you may ask him or her to pass it back to you.

TABLETOP TOUR

Every time you dine, you will be provided with a unique place setting that reflects the menu and level of formality of the occasion. The information below will help you to navigate a formal place setting, a good place to start because everything else will seem easy after you master this.

PLACE SETTINGS

Don't know your way around a place setting? Then concentrate on the **big** picture as you navigate. The letters **BIG** will help you to remember the correct placement of dishes and glassware. Just as you read these letters from left to right, picture them superimposed left to right over your place setting as a map of your dining territory. Voila! Big solution!

B
on the left for
Bread plate

I
for In between

G
on the right
for Glassware

Napkin

- Take your napkin from the table and place it in your lap once your host has done so. At a meal without a host, place it in your lap soon after you are seated and before touching anything else on your place setting. It remains in your lap throughout your meal.

- Unfold the napkin below the edge of the table; don't flap it open in midair. A small tea or luncheon napkin is unfolded completely, while a large dinner napkin remains folded in half with the fold toward your waist.

- Don't tuck a napkin into your collar or shirt front unless you are dining in a specialty restaurant where this is encouraged.

- Use your napkin for two tasks only: to clean your fingertips throughout the meal and to *blot* (not wipe) your mouth. Never use it to wipe your face, touch your nose, or clean glassware or utensils.

- If you drop your napkin in a restaurant, don't pick it up from the floor. Ask the server for another. If it happens when dining in someone's home, pick it up.

- Never place food that you have removed from your mouth (egg shell, olive pit, fish bone, gristle) into your napkin. Place it on the side of a plate.

- Place the napkin on the table at the left side of your place setting, soiled side down, if you leave the table temporarily and at the end of the meal. You don't have to refold it completely, but gather it in loose folds. If there is a host, he or she does this first to indicate the end of the meal.

- In a restaurant, you may request a dark napkin if you are wearing dark clothing and want to avoid lint from a white napkin.

Service Plate

The service plate, or base plate, is normally in the center of your place setting when you sit down. It is not the plate that your food will be served on. It may hold your napkin, a program for the event, or a menu card. Place the napkin in your lap and the menu card or program to one side or above your plate. The server either will place the first course onto this service plate or will remove it before serving the first course.

Utensils

In most restaurants today, a minimum number of utensils will be on the table when you sit down, and all other pieces will arrive with specific dishes that you order. For banquet settings, utensils are arranged on the table in the order in which you will use them, moving from the outside in toward the service plate. Forks are placed to the left of the plate and knives and spoons to the right. If you see a fork and spoon placed above your plate, they are for dessert. You may receive additional unique utensils as various courses are served.

To decide which utensil to use for each course, study your place setting and use pieces on the outside first and move in toward the center. You may also follow the lead of your host or table companions. Take your time and watch others when you are uncertain.

- Never use your own utensil in a serving dish.
- Utensils that have been used should not be placed back on the table, tablecloth, or placemat. Why? They're dirty.
- If you drop a utensil (or anything else), don't dive under the table to retrieve it. Ask the server or your host for another.
- The entire bowl of a spoon or bed of a fork does not go into your mouth.
- A knife never goes in or near your mouth.
- Don't gesture with utensils when in conversation.
- Never extend a pinkie finger when using a utensil or drinking from a cup.

Glassware

Glasses are placed above and to the right of the service plate in the order they will be used. In most restaurants today, only a water glass is placed on the table before you order specific beverages. At catered luncheons and dinners and at meals in private homes, you will find some of the glasses mentioned below at your place setting when you sit down.

- **sherry** small stem; served with soup course (rarely used today)

- **white wine** medium-size stem

- **red wine** large stem

- **water** placed above the knife or slightly behind the wine glasses

- **champagne** narrow flute; placed to the right or behind water glass; served with dessert

General Glassware Guidelines

- White wine, red wine, and champagne glasses are held by the stem.

- Never extend a pinkie finger when drinking from a glass.

- Don't turn over a glass to indicate that you do not wish to receive that beverage Simply say, "No, thank you," to the server.

- If you receive a smudged glass, don't attempt to clean it with your napkin. Ask your server for another glass. When dining in a private home, smile and ignore it.

- Before drinking from a glass, blot your mouth with your napkin.

- Don't hold a glass up as a signal to a waiter that you need a beverage refill.

- Don't clink glasses during a toast at a business function.

- Raise your glass in front of you.

Bread Plate

This is set to the upper *left* side of your service plate (remember **BIG**). If your dining companion uses your bread plate, don't call attention to the error. Discreetly ask the server for another plate or place your bread on your salad or dinner plate.

Using your butter spreader (or the knife for the current course), take butter from a serving dish and place it on your bread plate before spreading it on your roll or bread. *Break* your bread or roll—*don't cut it*—one small piece at a time, and butter it while holding it over your bread plate.

Soup Plate, Bowl, or Cup

Soup is served in a large, shallow soup plate or in a bowl or cup with a saucer beneath.

Sit up relatively straight while the spoon travels up to your mouth. Soup comes to you; don't go to the soup. (This is why you sit close to the table, with no more than six to eight inches between your abdomen and the edge of the table.) Picture a soup plate as the face of a clock and dip your soup spoon in at the top of the plate (twelve o'clock), dipping away from yourself. Draw the bottom of the spoon over the rim of the plate to prevent drips.

When the level of the soup remaining in a soup plate is shallow and your spoon will scrape the bottom, you may tip the soup plate away from you by lifting the rim nearest to you (six o'clock) and spooning the soup away from you. Don't tip a soup bowl or cup in this manner.

Don't put the entire spoon into your mouth. Sip cream soup or broth from the spoon edge that faces you. The tip of the spoon comes to your mouth only when you are eating soup meat, vegetables, or noodles.

You may leave your spoon in your soup plate between bites and when you finish, but never leave a spoon in a smaller soup bowl or cup. Place it on the saucer beneath when resting and when finished.

When soup is served in a cup with one or two handles with a saucer beneath, you may begin to eat the soup with a spoon and finish by picking up the cup by one handle or both handles and drinking it.

Don't slurp your soup unless dining in a culture where it is expected.

Cup and Saucer

Never extend a pinkie finger when drinking from a cup. When drinking from a teacup, pinch the cup handle between you thumb and first two fingers. When drinking from a coffee cup or mug, place your index finger through a cup handle. Support the cup by placing your thumb on top of the handle and your middle finger under the handle. Don't wrap your hand completely around a cup or mug unless it has no handles.

Don't make noise with your spoon while stirring in a cup, and never leave a spoon in a cup. After stirring, place the spoon on the saucer or another plate, not on the table, tablecloth, or placemat.

Don't turn over a tea or coffee cup to indicate that you do not wish to receive that beverage. Simply say, "No, thank you," to the server.

Salt and Pepper

Don't add salt and pepper (or any condiment) to your food before tasting it. Always pass the salt and pepper containers together, never one without the other. When you pass them, place them on the table next to you, not into the hand of the next diner.

DINING STYLES

As you dine on formal occasions or with colleagues from other cultures, you will observe that not everyone uses utensils in the same manner, and, in fact, some diners use no utensils at all. Styles and practices differ greatly around the globe. Dining information provided below relates to Western dining. As you strive to become a global citizen, research and practice other styles as well so that you will be comfortable and confident in any dining environment.

AMERICAN STYLE

- Hold the knife in your right hand, and place your index finger where the handle meets the knife blade. This provides leverage for cutting.

- Cut food in one direction only by drawing the knife toward you; do not use a back-and-forth, sawing motion.

- Hold the fork, tines down, in your left hand and place your index finger on the back of the fork at the joint of the top and the handle.

- Cut only one piece of food at a time.

- After cutting, place the knife on the upper right edge of your plate with the blade facing into the center of the plate.

- Move the fork to your right hand (left-handed diners may keep the fork in their left hand) and hold it like a pencil. Move your fork to your mouth, not vice versa.

- Place utensils on the plate when not in use, not on the table, tablecloth, or placemat.

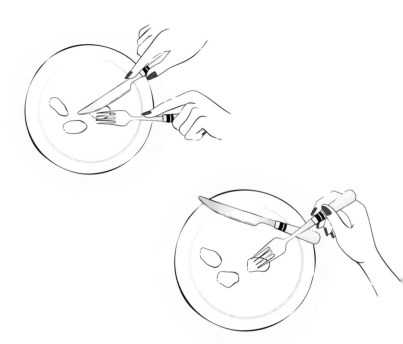

Silent Service Code

There are visual cues called the Silent Service Code that signal servers when you have finished a course or your meal. Visualize your plate as the face of a clock and place your utensils according to these guidelines to indicate the progress of your meal.

Rest Position

The fork is placed in the four o'clock position (handle pointing to four, if your plate were the face of a clock), and the knife is placed on the upper right edge of the plate with the blade facing in toward the center. Leave space between these two utensils. Use this position when you are talking, drinking, using your napkin, or if you leave the table temporarily and want to finish this course when you return.

Finished Position

When you have finished a course or the meal, place your fork and knife side-by-side in the four o'clock position. The tines of the fork are pointed *up* and the cutting edge of the knife faces the center of the plate.

EUROPEAN STYLE

- Use the fork in your left hand (with your index finger on the back of the fork at the joint of the top and the handle) to hold food in place while the knife in your right hand *cuts one piece of food at a time*. This rule is the same for right- and left-handed diners.

- Leave the fork in your left hand, tines down, and bring food to your mouth by pivoting your wrist and raising your forearm.

- You may use the knife, which remains in your right hand, to push small portions of food onto the tines of the fork.

- When eating food that cannot be pierced by a fork, put your knife down and use the fork in your predominant hand to scoop food and bring it to your mouth. Or turn the fork over, hold it like a pencil in your left hand, use your knife to move food onto the bed of the fork, and move the food to your mouth. This will take some practice.

- Place utensils on the plate when not in use, not on the table, tablecloth, or placemat. Used utensils should never be placed on the table.

Silent Service Code

Remember that there are signals you can send to indicate that you have finished a course or your meal. When using the European dining style, these signals differ slightly from the American style.

Rest Position

The knife is placed with its handle pointing to the four o'clock position. The fork, with its tines down and handle pointing toward the eight o'clock position, is placed overlapping the knife blade, creating an X on the plate. Use this position when you are talking, drinking, using your napkin, or when you leave the table temporarily.

Finished Position

When you have finished a course or the meal, place your fork and knife together in the four o'clock position. The tines of the fork are pointed *down* and the cutting edge of the knife is facing the center of the plate.

RESTAURANT DINING

Restaurant dining choices today include family-friendly chains, sidewalk bistros, all-you-can-eat buffets, coffee shops, fast food and carryouts, ethnic cafes, sports bars, and five-star establishments. Whew! So many choices of style and menu, but they all have one thing in common, and that is that diners need to arrive not only with cash or credit card but with their manners, as well, in order to ensure a pleasant experience. And manners are a two-way street in restaurant dining. Management and staff have an obligation to serve a large helping of courtesy along with food and beverages.

CHECKLIST: Servers Speak Up

Ever wonder what restaurant staff think of their customers' manners? The following mistakes appear consistently on servers' lists of pet peeves:

* talking on cell phones and ignoring servers when they appear at the table

* loud and demanding individuals who feel they are entitled to more attention than other diners

* extreme impatience

* displaying a condescending attitude toward staff

* failing to listen to information provided

* using a server's name too many times in an attempt to manipulate them

* calling out loudly, snapping fingers, or waving frantically to get a server's attention, when a raised hand is sufficient

* showing off to fellow diners by criticizing a server

* directing anger or disappointment about food to the server—he or she didn't cook it

* failing to thank a server at least once during meal service (it is not necessary to say thank you every time an item is served or cleared)

* failing to supervise children— noise, extraordinary messiness, and failing to keep them seated

* eating a substantial portion of a dish or course and then registering a complaint about it

* scraping or stacking plates when finished eating

CUSTOMER COURTESY

There's an old saying that one can learn a lot about a person by watching him eat. Is he patient, generous, neat, capable of sharing, mindful of the needs of others, and does he display gratitude and appreciation?

When dining in a restaurant, if someone's behavior changes between speaking with their companions and speaking with servers and staff, they have opened a window into their character. What we see when they are rude to staff is their true nature. Those who demonstrate kindness and respect to all are genuinely courteous.

À LA CARTE COURTESY

You will improve your restaurant dining experience when you begin with these basic behavior modifications:

- If you make a reservation and your plans change, call to cancel. It is extremely rude not to do so. No-show diners make a significant economic impact on a restaurant.

- Arrive on time for a reservation or call ahead to discuss your ETA. Running late? Most restaurants will hold a reservation for up to twenty minutes for late arrivals, but each has its own policy. Call to check. It may not be possible for yours to seat you if you arrive substantially later than the time of your reservation.

- If you miss the call that your table is ready because you left the waiting area, it's your fault. When you return, you can politely discuss the situation with the host or hostess and explore your options. It's rude to complain.

- Complaining makes others uncomfortable. If there is a problem with your food or your order is incorrect, politely point it out to the server so that it can be corrected. Invite companions to begin eating while you wait for a correction to be made.

- If timing is off and your companion's food arrives before yours, encourage him or her to begin. If yours arrives before his or hers, stall before beginning to eat or ask the waiter to hold your meal until all can be served.

- Attention, campers! It's rude to camp at your table after your meal. A brief wrap-up session following dessert is acceptable, but a filibuster is not. Others may be waiting to be seated, and restaurants rely on multiple seatings at each meal to be profitable.

- Speak to management if noise from other diners disturbs you, not to the diners themselves.

ORDER UP

When it's your turn to order, follow these rules and you will shine when you dine:

- As a guest, you may be invited to order first. It's OK to stall for time; pass the baton. Ask others at the table what they recommend to help you determine the number of courses you should order. Try to order the same number of courses as your dining companions. It's uncomfortable to eat a course alone.

- When you're a guest, don't order the most expensive items on the menu.

- Never be the first person to order alcohol.

- Order food that you know how to eat. Avoid messy, challenging items.

- Don't ask the waiter to describe *every* ingredient in several dishes you are considering unless you have serious food allergies. It is a good idea to check the restaurant menu online and call ahead with your questions.

- When dining in an ethnic restaurant with unfamiliar cuisine, never hesitate to ask others for advice on what to order and how to proceed. Smile and be eager to learn.

KIDS' TABLE

Define the rules of restaurant behavior to your children in advance. Table manners are taught at home and refined when dining out. Children can't behave appropriately without guidance, so share your expectations. There are too many distractions in a restaurant for a young child to be able to focus on rules presented there.

- Supervise children. They should not be permitted to leave the table and roam through a dining room without an adult.

- Don't allow children to be excessively noisy, throw food or utensils, or stand in a booth and lean over the back to distract diners at an adjacent table.

- Never allow children to play with condiment containers or, worse, put them in their mouths.

- Teach children to be respectful to servers.

- Parents can set an example by demonstrating their table manners.

CHECKLIST: Management Manners

Continuing the quest to improve dining experiences in both front and back of the house, we turn to restaurant management and staff. Your customers have completed their manners makeover, so it's time for you to review your courtesy quotient. Here are comments from customers that will help you to comply:

* Take reasonable steps to ensure that all diners have a positive and comfortable experience.

* Don't think diners are idiots. Your attitude shows.

* Too much information can be overload. Reading a list of seven specials with eight ingredients each is not only pretentious, it's unmanageable for staff and customers.

* Remind your staff in the reception area that they are the face of your restaurant, your first impression. What they do and say will affect a diner's attitude and dining experience. They should be trained to *smile* and to be attentive, friendly, and flexible. Diners don't want to hear corporate policy quoted when they really just want to interact with a human being.

CHEZ GERM

Diners are particularly concerned about cleanliness and want to see visible signs that an establishment is taking extraordinary measures to ensure the health and safety of the facility, equipment, furniture, service, and food.

* Diners want to see plastic gloves on more hands and more hand sanitizer dispensers.

* Don't permit staff to work when they are ill.

* Sanitizing tables does not mean wiping them down with dirty rags or sponges.

* Clean condiment containers several times each day.

* Regularly scrub the walls and partitions that separate booths.

* Wipe down and sanitize high chairs and booster seats after each use.

FAST-FOOD FINESSE

Do you want manners with that? Yes, we do, even when dining in a fast-food establishment. Courtesy is expected on both sides of the counter.

FAST-DINING GUESTS

- Treat all staff with respect.
- Step out of line if you haven't decided what to order by the time you reach the counter attendant.
- When waiting for your order, step to the side of the line.
- Supervise children.
- Be frugal with condiments and napkins.
- Clean up after yourself—table and chair or bench. Report major spills to a staff member.
- Keep noise to a minimum at your table.
- When taking a cup lid, try not to touch more than the top lid in the stack.
- Don't touch the serving tip of condiment dispensers.

MANAGEMENT AND STAFF

- Treat customers with respect.
- Smile and make eye contact. Not only is it your first impression, but it can affect a customer's experience.
- Listen carefully and repeat items ordered.
- Hands should be clean, no long fingernails, hair covered. No piercings on the tongue, lips, cheeks, or eyebrows. Don't touch your face or hair while on duty. No gum chewing.
- Clean the tables often. Fast-food diners are used to bussing their own tables, but they don't want to have to clean a table before sitting down.

DRIVE-THROUGH RUDENESS

- Be courteous to employees. A *please* and *thank you* go a long way.
- Pay attention when in line and move your car up quickly as space opens in front of you.
- When it's your turn to order, put down your cell phone and turn down your radio.

CHECKLIST: Server Misdeeds

Attention, servers! Your customers want you to **stop**

* writing your name in crayon on their table;

* kneeling or squatting down next to the table to introduce yourself;

* eating or drinking in areas where they can see you;

* touching your head or face, or scratching anything;

* complaining about customers in areas where you can be heard;

* stating your personal favorite menu item or special unless you are asked;

* saying "an excellent choice" after a diner has ordered;

* clearing a plate or course before all diners at the table have finished;

* spraying tables with cleaning solution, sending a smelly cloud to adjacent tables; and

* asking customers if they want change when they pay their check in cash.

• Place your order quickly and speak clearly. Don't allow young children to place the order. They are often difficult to understand through the microphone and headset.

• Turn off windshield wipers when at the cashier and pick-up windows.

• Have your money ready when you arrive at the cashier window.

• Don't add to or change your order when you arrive at the cashier or pick-up window.

• After receiving your order, don't hold up the line to check it. A quick glance into your bag is one thing; a deep dive is another. Pull into a parking spot or into the area that is designated for this purpose.

- Don't distribute food to others in the car while stopped at the pick-up window.
- Night run? Turn off headlights if there is a car in line in front of you.
- Tipping is not expected or required.
- Ordering for your entire office, extended family, or Little League team? Please, go inside to place the order.

FOOD-TRUCK FAUX PAS

Are you a food-truck foodie? One of *the* hottest trends today, food trucks pull up with not only creative and delicious food but with their own etiquette as well. The rules aren't posted like the menu, so owners and chefs share their expectations through blogs and other social media.

Don't hold up the line. Study the menu while you wait in line, not when you arrive at the order window. Text or email your order whenever you can. Holding a place in line for others is rude. Don't ask for many additions or subtractions to advertised menu items. If you are vegan with a peanut and gluten allergy thrown in, don't try to mold the menu to fit your needs. Find another truck. If substitutions are permitted, write down your order on a slip of paper and give it to the server.

Be patient. Displaying an attitude and body language that indicate that you are too important to wait in line will not endear you to the owner or server.

Neatness counts. Clean up after yourself. Getting supplies or condiments from one truck after purchasing food from another truck is tacky.

Exact change is appreciated, as are small bills. Tipping is also appreciated. It doesn't have to be at the 15–20-percent level as in a restaurant, but be generous.

COFFEE SHOPS

Step out of line if you haven't decided what to order by the time you get to the head of the line. Nobody wants to stand behind you while you read the wall-mounted menu or change your order three times.

If you are placing a large order for beverages with a multitude of ingredients and tweaks, write down the order and hand it to the cashier or barista.

Supervise children as they pass open shelves of food items. Even though all things are wrapped, it's not appetizing to watch little hands poke, prod, and squeeze everything within their reach. Clean up after yourself at the sugar-and-cream station, and report major spills to an employee.

Don't put your feet on or spread your belongings on empty chairs, blocking their use by others. You've heard it before, so just don't do it: no setting up camp, parking your laptop, and settling in for the day . . . unless you are prepared to purchase something about every two hours. Remember, you are using resources of the business while sitting there and taking up space that other paying customers might occupy.

FOOD-SERVICE GLOSSARY

How food is served can dictate decorum. Let's take a look at several types of food service and their unique etiquette rules.

BUFFET

A display of prepared food from which diners serve themselves—diners encounter this type of dining experience often, at cocktail receptions, business meetings, weddings, school and neighborhood gatherings, and in restaurant settings. Because

the display area and serving pieces are shared by many people, it is particularly important to follow not only basic rules of courtesy, but of hygiene as well.

- Wash your hands or use hand sanitizer before entering a buffet line. You will be touching serving utensils that others have touched or will touch.

- Don't carry your main course plate and dessert plate away from the serving table at the same time. Go back for your dessert after you have finished the main course.

- Don't taste or eat food directly from the serving dishes. Place food items on your plate, move away from the buffet, and then begin to eat.

- Don't eat from your own plate while standing in the serving line.

- Don't use fingers to pick up anything from a buffet unless food is bite-size and there are no serving utensils.

- Don't take too much food. Think of others behind you in line. Return for a second helping if you are still hungry after your first serving.

- After you have served yourself, don't stand at the serving table and talk with others. Serve yourself, and move away.

- Always get a fresh plate when returning to a buffet for more food. Do not reuse your plate, unless you are in someone's home and there are no extras.

- Don't move tongs, spoons, or other serving pieces to different serving bowls, pans, or containers. You may cross-contaminate food and affect diners who have food allergies

- Never cough or sneeze while serving yourself from a buffet. If the urge for either comes on, leave the line.

- Don't stand too close to others in line.

- Help children to avoid messes and control portions.

- You may begin eating as soon as you reach your seat.

- Don't attempt to take food home from a restaurant buffet.

- Tipping is necessary but not at the 20-percent level. Tip $1–$2 per person if the staff is only clearing plates; 10 percent of the total bill if they also provide beverage service.

QUICK TIP
Don't Follow Your Nose

Imagine you are standing in line at a cafeteria soup station and just watched a patron raise the soup ladle to within an inch of her nose to smell the soup. She then grimaces and lowers the ladle to the serving crock, evidently not pleased with what she has sniffed. She then leaves the line in search of other lunch options, as do the five people, including you, in line behind her, who have suddenly lost their appetite for soup. Don't be that person! It's bad enough that hundreds of hands touch the serving utensils in buffets and cafeterias every day, but please, no noses.

POTLUCK PARTICULARS

See also the "Buffet" section on page 185.

Host

- Consider placing food on more than one table in order to facilitate serving.

- Have lots of napkins available and cleaning supplies handy for spills, and don't make a big deal out of accidents—it may embarrass a guest.

- Keep a list of foods that will be needed: apps, sides, main dishes, and options for vegetarian, vegan, or gluten-free diners. Other contributions needed include paper and plastic products, beverages, and snacks.

- If oven and refrigerator space is limited, let guests know in advance.

Guest

- Don't attend without making a contribution to the menu or supplies.

- Play it safe and don't bring anything that contains nuts. Dishes that do contain nuts should be labelled and set on a separate serving table.

- Store-bought food is OK.

- Don't change your contribution category without notifying the host.

- Follow instructions on what quantity to bring—enough to feed four or eight?

- Don't assume that you will be able to reheat or refrigerate your dish when you arrive. An exception is something that will be grilled just before serving, but this information will be provided to you in advance.

- It is a good idea to label your dish by name and ingredients. Make a small sign and place it beside your contribution.

- If you'll be arriving late to the party, don't sign up to bring an appetizer. If you are bringing dessert and have to leave the party early, bring it in a disposable container.

- Follow safe food-handling guidelines for refrigeration, etc.

- Bring a serving utensil and potholder or trivet to place under a hot dish. Label your serving dish, utensils, and other equipment with your name. If the gathering is informal, use a disposable container with disposable utensils.

- Take small portions so that you leave as much as possible for other guests.

- Help children to avoid messes and control portions.

- You may begin eating as soon as you reach your seat.

- Bring a bag to carry home your dirty serving dish. You may not be able to use the host's kitchen sink to give it a rinse before heading home.
- If you don't want to take your leftovers, bring a few small plastic containers to put them in, and offer them to your host or other guests.
- Help the host with setup, maintaining table, and cleanup.
- Don't criticize dishes that have been contributed.
- Offer your host the remaining food from your serving dish. If he or she declines, you may take home your leftovers. Don't take leftovers from someone else's contribution without an offer from your host or the guest who brought it.

Family-Style Service
Prepared food is placed on shared serving plates and platters for guests to share. This is the type of food service in private homes, etc.

French Service
At formal dinners, food on a large tray is presented to each table by a server. A guest indicates to the server what he or she would like to eat, and the server places a portion of those foods from the tray onto the diner's plate. A second server may follow with side dishes and sauces.

Russian Service
This is also a formal dinner service. A server brings a large tray of food to the table and presents it to each diner. Each diner serves himself from the tray using the serving utensils provided. A second server may follow with side dishes and sauces, and diners serve themselves. (Ask the server for help if you are unable to serve yourself for any reason.) Don't take more than a single portion of food from the tray.

TAPAS
A variety of small plates served to the table for all diners to taste and share. At some tapas bars, the food is served buffet style and diners take what they want and tell the bartender or server what they had. At others, the bartender or server will place the items on a diner's plate. Just watch, wait, and ask questions when unsure.
- Don't eat directly from the serving plates. Don't take the last item from a serving plate without asking if others want to share.
- Don't dip your bread into the sauce on a shared serving plate.
- If items are served on toothpicks, keep the empty toothpicks on your plate. They may be how your bill is tallied later.

Tipping Pointers

At the end of the meal, when determining how much to tip a server, separate your dining experience into two categories—one for the service you received and the other for the quality of the food—and create a mental report card for each. You should determine how much to tip a server based on the service category only. Don't hold a server responsible for the quality of the food. When you have an issue with quality, share your concern with management.

To make a show of tipping is tacky. Don't brag about how much you are tipping, flaunt the tip, present it with too grand a gesture, or say something about it to the server.

If you are using a gift certificate or discount coupon to pay for your meal, your tip should be based on the full price of the meal, not on what you are paying out of pocket.

Including coins as part of a tip is OK, as long as it is not done as a slight to the server.

TIPPING GUIDELINES

Servers 15 percent (reasonable service) to 20 percent (exceptional service)

Sommelier 10–15 percent of the price of the wine consumed, if exceptional service was provided. Give the tip to the manager or directly to the sommelier.

Coat Check Usually $1 per coat or item.

Valet Parking Attendants $2–$5 is the norm.

CHAPTER 11

DOWN THE AISLE

You're engaged! Congratulations and best wishes! The months ahead will take you on one of the most memorable adventures of your life. Don't let the stress of planning the big event cause you to lose your sense and sensibility or send relationships with family and friends spinning out of control. One of the most useful navigational tools to keep a wedding couple on track is etiquette—plain and simple. Rely on wedding etiquette rules and traditions as a foundation, and then build on it in your own way.

If the word *etiquette* overwhelms you, think of it as a trusty friend with advice on many of the questions that will arise as you plan your special event. You will consult this friend for guidance, hear about what others have done before you, and then make your own decisions on how to proceed to put your stamp on the day.

Etiquette rules and traditions presented in this chapter are meant to serve as a resource on how things have been done in the past, how they might be done at your wedding if you fancy the suggestions; or how they could be revised or ignored with good reason. Etiquette traditions will help you to think about all of the possibilities before making decisions.

DETERMINE YOUR VISION

To ensure that your dream wedding does not turn into a nightmare, begin the planning process with an exercise for you and your intended on day two of your engagement. Without discussion, each of you will write a list of what will make the perfect wedding day for you. Then compare notes. Does your list include a gathering of three hundred of your nearest and dearest at an extravagant cathedral wedding and reception, while your partner's list describes a handful of family and friends in attendance as you exchange vows under the oak tree where you shared your first kiss? Better to discover this discrepancy early, before you head down the road assuming that you know what your partner wants. It will be easier to find common ground at the beginning of the process than three months later when you have to put on the brakes and make a major course correction. If you do find yourselves with polar-opposite visions, try to begin to find the middle ground. This is not an I-win–you-lose situation.

Part two of this planning exercise is to go back to your lists, again with no collaboration, and highlight your wedding must-haves. Compare notes again. Now is the time to begin the give-and-take negotiation that will lead to a win-win wedding: I'll trade you fifty guests for a champagne fountain and a box of live butterflies. This gentle tug-of-war will result in a consolidated vision of your perfect day. Neither of you will end up with everything on your original list, but your combined list will have you moving in the same direction. And once you agree on your vision, other things will fall into place more easily.

TIMELINE

Whether you have eighteen months to create your wedding or three, you need to establish a planning timeline as soon as your wedding date is set. It will help you to stay focused, track components of your event, nudge yourself and vendors, and steer clear of last-minute crises. Once your wedding date is set, start to count backward from that date and insert target goals at various intervals.

Setting the Date Check your target date and one or two backup dates with family members and your immediate circle of friends. Next, check the events calendar of the city or community in which the ceremony will take place to avoid dates of marathons, outdoor festivals, political conventions, or other traffic-snarling, hotel-hogging events that could compete with your plans.

Establishing a Timeline Create a reverse planning schedule, counting backward from your target date. Presented here is a typical timeline for a wedding with a one-year planning period. Allot

- six to twelve months for booking a popular site;
- six to eight months for securing your favorite caterer, florist, photographer, DJ, and other vendors on a Saturday in June;
- six to eight months ahead for sending a save-the-date announcement for a destination wedding; four to five months for a wedding in your city of residence;

- eight to twelve weeks for mailing invitations (or earlier if you have not mailed a save-the-date announcement), and don't forget to include additional time for selection, design, printing, and addressing;
- four to six weeks ahead for the RSVP deadline.

If you are planning a small wedding, you can accomplish these steps in less time, so shrink those windows accordingly. When selecting your date, the most important question to ask is, are you giving yourself enough time to produce the wedding that you envision?

SAVE-THE-DATE ANNOUNCEMENTS

Many couples choose to create and send a save-the-date announcement which precedes the mailing of the wedding invitation by several months. A longer lead time is required for destination weddings or weddings planned on or near a major holiday.

Before You Print A number of decisions must be made prior to mailing this announcement—date, location, the number of guests you can afford and that the venue can accommodate, wedding website created (may not be complete at this stage), and a final guest list. Everyone who receives a save the date must receive the official invitation. You cannot, in good conscience, un-invite a guest who has received this piece without causing irreparable damage to a relationship.

Design The first impression of your wedding will come from your save-the-date announcement, so plan and create it wisely. It is a good idea if the design of this first piece matches the design of your invitations, so that you brand your event in its early stages. But in the interest of speed, and perhaps the limits of budget, it may not be possible. A postcard can serve the same purpose.

Guests The save the date should carry the *specifics* of who's invited, as will the official invitation. Now is the time to manage expectations. Are you including plus ones? Children? Address the announcements carefully: Mr. and Mrs., Mr. and Ms., Ms. and Ms., Mr. and Mr., Mr. and Guest, Ms. and Guest, Mr. and Mrs. and family?

Gift Information No mention of gifts or a registry should be made on this piece. It may, however, contain a wedding website address where guests can find wedding details including gift registry information.

INVITATIONS
· · · · · · · · · · · · · · · ·

There are no absolute "rights" or "wrongs" for wedding invitation design or content. You are limited only by your imagination and budget. Let's look at traditional styles and sample text as a starting point.

TEXT

The couple's circumstances (who is paying for the wedding, previous marital status, family relations) may influence the text of a wedding invitation. General rules to apply for a formal invitation include:

- Use complete names, not initials or nicknames. Roman numerals following a surname are acceptable.
- The bride's last name is used on an invitation only if
  - it is different from the last name of her parents, if they are issuing the invitation;
  - the bride and the groom are extending the invitation themselves; or
  - the bride holds military rank.
- For formal weddings, spell out the hour, date, and year, and don't use *a.m.* or *p.m.*, but rather *o'clock* following the hour:

Saturday, the tenth of September
two thousand and eighteen
at four o'clock

- Don't use abbreviations (spell out *Street* or *Avenue*). Numerals are used in the street address of the wedding site for clarity:

111 Main Street, not *One eleven Main Street*

- The British spelling of *honour* and *favour* are acceptable, but most couples now use *honor* and *favor*.

- The term *honor of your presence* is normally used when a wedding will take place in a church, synagogue, or other house of worship, while the term *pleasure of your company* is used when the service is held in a home, club, hotel, or other nonreligious site.

SAMPLE TEXT

The text of the invitation is *not* automatically determined by who is paying for the wedding. For example, if the bride resides primarily with her mother and stepfather and her biological father is paying for the wedding, the mother's and stepfather's names appear on the invitation as hosts. If the bride has been close to both parents and her stepfather, she may wish to include all three names on the invitation, but this is her decision to do so.

TRADITIONAL WEDDING INVITATION:

Mr. and Mrs. Parker Watson Jones
request the honor of your presence
at the marriage of their daughter
Elizabeth Jane
to
Mr. Stephen Allan Franklin
on Saturday, the tenth of August
two thousand and nineteen
at four o'clock
Saint Agnes Cathedral
845 Mission Bay Parkway
San Francisco

A separate reception invitation card would accompany the invitation above:

Reception (or *Luncheon* or *Dinner*)
immediately following the ceremony
Community Country Club
2056 Wilkins Boulevard
San Francisco

If the wedding and reception will take place in the same location, the text can be combined:

Mr. and Mrs. Parker Watson Jones
request the pleasure of your company
at the marriage of their daughter
Elizabeth Jane
to
Mr. Stephen Allan Franklin
on Saturday, the tenth of August
two thousand and nineteen
at four o'clock
and at dinner
immediately following the ceremony
The Ritz Carlton Hotel
845 Mission Bay Parkway
San Francisco

The appropriate honorific precedes a public dignitary's name on a wedding invitation:

The Honorable Eleanor Alice Norton
and Mr. John Hastings Norton
request the pleasure of your company
at the marriage of their daughter . . .
or
The Honorable William Parker Finnigan
and Mrs. Finnigan
request the honor of your presence
at the marriage of their daughter . . .

When parents are divorced and the mother has not remarried:

Mrs. Lorraine Wallace Smith*
Mr. Michael Kennington Smith
request the pleasure of your company
at the marriage of their daughter
Leslie Anne
to
Mr. Michael Allen Watkins . . .

* The absence of *and* between the parents' names indicates that they are divorced.

Divorced parents who have remarried (different last names indicate that they have remarried):

Mrs. Lorraine Wallace Atkins
Mr. Michael Kennington Smith
request the pleasure of your company
at the marriage of their daughter
Leslie Anne Smith
to
Mr. Michael Allen Watkins . . .

Married parents who use different last names:

Ms. Anne Marie Wilson
and Mr. Michael Kennington Smith*
request the pleasure of your company
at the marriage of their daughter
Leslie Anne Smith
to
Mr. Michael Allen Watkins . . .

* The *and* between the hosts' names indicates that they are a married couple.

If the bride's mother is a widow who has remarried, or if she is divorced:

Mr. and Mrs. William Parker Johnston
request the pleasure of your company
at the marriage of Mrs. Johnston's daughter
Leslie Anne Miller
to
Mr. Michael Allen Watkins . . .

For a wedding couple giving their own wedding:

Sallie Elizabeth Jeffries
and
Emily Ann Benson
request the pleasure of your company . . .
or
The honor of your presence
is requested at the marriage of
Michael Howard Logan
and
William Thomas Ketting . . .

If you are postponing a wedding:

Mr. and Mrs. David Smith
announce that the marriage of their daughter
Mary Ann
to
Mr. John Edward Wells
has been postponed from
Saturday, the tenth of April
to
Saturday, the twentieth of September
two thousand and eighteen
at five o'clock
Saint Andrews Congregation
1050 Prince Street
Alexandria, Virginia

For canceling a wedding:

Mr. and Mrs. David Smith
announce that the marriage of their daughter
Rachel Marie
to
Mr. Allan Michael Hudson
by mutual agreement
will not take place

FORMS OF ADDRESS

If the wedding budget permits, hire a calligrapher to address both the inside and carrier envelopes for the invitations. If not, use an attractive computer font or ask a friend or relative to assist with hand addressing. Many invitation vendors offer addressing for an additional fee. Please, no mailing labels.

Guest	Carrier Envelope	Inside Envelope
Married couple	Mr. and Mrs. James F. Hatch	Mr. and Mrs. Hatch
Married couple, including a military officer	General James F. Hatch and Mrs. Hatch	General and Mrs. Hatch
Married couple with different last names	Mr. Charles Olson and Ms. Mary Smith	Mr. Olson and Ms. Smith
Unmarried couple (list first the name of the person you know better)	Ms. Janet Renninger and Mr. Larry Patterson	Ms. Renninger and Mr. Patterson
Guest plus one	Mr. David Kellogg	Mr. David Kellogg and Guest
Couple plus children	Mr. and Mrs. Jacob Stein	Mr. and Mrs. Stein Amy, Lea, and Hannah
Couple and entire family (proceed with caution)	Mr. and Mrs. Jay Gordon	Mr. and Mrs. Gordon and Family
Same-sex couple (list first the name of the person you know better)	Mr. Adam Jordan and Mr. George Benson	Mr. Jordan and Mr. Benson or Mr. Jordan and Mr. Benson

DESIGN

The sky's the limit on invitation design, but rely on traditional design and text as a launchpad. The standard white or ivory invitation on heavy card stock (folded or unfolded) remains the preferred design for the majority of couples. The wedding budget will dictate whether or not the invitation is produced by engraving, letterpress, or flat printing.

Accompanying pieces may include:

- reception invitation
- response card and return envelope
- driving instructions or map
- hotel information
- inside envelope to hold the invitation, and carrier (outside) envelope

INVITATION ASSEMBLY

A wedding invitation may include up to four pieces and three envelopes, and should be assembled carefully for mailing. While holding the *inside* envelope with its back facing you, flap up, the inserts will build out toward you as follows:

- invitation with printed side facing you
- reception invitation
- driving instructions or map
- response card tucked under the flap of the response envelope
- fold down the flap of the inside envelope, but do *not* seal or tuck it

Insert the inner envelope and its contents into the larger carrier envelope with the front of the inner envelope facing the back of the carrier envelope.

MAILING

Take one complete package to the post office for weighing. Buy the appropriate stamps based on the total weight. Use postage stamps; never use a postal meter for a wedding invitation! Place a stamp on the return envelope. Ask the post office to cancel envelopes by hand to avoid machine processing that might result in damage or overprinting. Most will comply.

Mail your invitations at least eight to twelve weeks before the wedding. Mail an invitation to yourself to find out how long it takes for delivery.

RESPONDING TO A WEDDING INVITATION

Always respond to a wedding invitation quickly, and at least no later than the deadline date. It is imperative that the wedding couple know the number of guests to expect at least three to four weeks before the wedding date. Don't ask if you may bring a guest if your invitation is addressed to you only.

If no response card is provided, compose a handwritten note, using the wedding invitation as a template for your response:

Mr. and Mrs. Henry Abbott Fisher
accept with pleasure
the kind invitation of
Mr. and Mrs. Patrick Olson Smith
for Saturday, the tenth of April
Or,
Mr. and Mrs. Henry Abbott Fisher
sincerely regret that
due to an illness in their family
they will be unable to accept
the kind invitation of
Mr. and Mrs. Patrick Olson Smith
for Saturday, the tenth of April

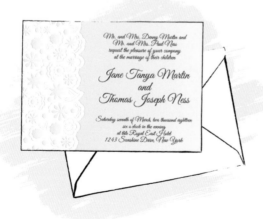

OLD SCHOOL VS. NEW SCHOOL
Wedding Expenses

Who pays for the wedding? That used to be an easy question to answer, because tradition dictated a specific breakdown of expenses and their assignment to either the bride's or groom's family. But today, many factors influence how a wedding will be funded—couple's families share expenses evenly, divorced parents or blended families contribute, the couple pays for their own wedding—which means that every line item in the budget will be discussed thoroughly before an assignment is made.

Historically, the breakdown of expenses was as listed below. Many of today's couples still follow these guidelines.

BRIDE AND/OR BRIDE'S FAMILY

- groom's ring
- bridesmaids' luncheon
- invitations, announcements, stationery, wedding programs, and thank-you notes
- calligraphy
- wedding gown and accessories, mother's and father's formalwear
- flowers for ceremony and reception; bouquets and corsages for bridesmaids and flower girls (but not for the bride)
- fee for use of church (or other wedding venue) and church support staff (organist, soloist, sexton, but not minister's fee)
- engagement and wedding photographs and video

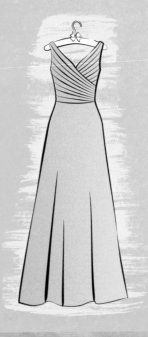

- transportation of the wedding party to the ceremony and reception
- food, beverages, decorations, and music and/or entertainment
- wedding gift for the groom and each bride's attendant

GROOM AND/OR GROOM'S FAMILY

- bride's engagement and wedding rings
- rehearsal dinner
- groom's formalwear and his family's formalwear
- bride's bouquet, boutonnieres for the men in the wedding party, corsages for the mothers and grandmothers
- marriage license
- officiant's fee
- limousine to the airport or hotel after reception
- honeymoon
- wedding gift for the bride and each of the groomsmen

CEREMONY

The order and content of wedding ceremonies differ greatly due to faith-based protocol, culture, community, family traditions, and personal preferences of the wedding couple. Below are general guidelines for a *traditional* wedding ceremony, offered as example only.

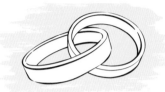

USHERS' ROLE

Ushers greet guests at the venue entrance and escort women to their seats, with their male companion walking behind. The bride's guests are seated on the left side of the sanctuary and groom's guests on the right. If far fewer guests of either the bride or the groom are able to attend, ushers evenly distribute guests on both sides of the aisle.

Front rows are reserved for family members. Ushers should be given a seating plan or instructions for placement of family and other special guests.

PROCESSIONAL

If using an aisle runner, ushers unroll the runner immediately before the processional begins and either return to the rear of church to take their places in the line of attendants or move to the front to stand with the groom.

The processional begins with the clergyman, groom, and best man entering from the side at the front of the church and taking their places at the altar, facing the congregation.

The wedding party advances down the aisle in the following order:
- ushers (who move to the right of the altar)
- bridesmaids (who move to the left of the altar)
- or bridesmaids and ushers walk together and split when they reach the altar
- maid of honor and/or matron of honor (who takes her place at what will be the bride's immediate left)
- flower girl and/or ring bearer (who may stand with the bridesmaids or ushers, respectively, or sit with their families after walking down the aisle)
- bride on her father's right arm

Variations

Faith-based protocol, space configuration, or personal preference may dictate variations on the processional:

- bride is accompanied by both parents; groom may be, as well
- groom walks his mother down the aisle to her seat and takes his place at the altar just before attendants start down the aisle
- same-sex couple chooses to walk together or individually with their parents

RECESSIONAL

- bride walks up aisle on the groom's right arm
- wedding party follows in reverse order of processional
- clergyman exits at side front
- guests leave seats starting with front rows; ushers may assist by standing at the side of the rows to release guests

RECEPTION
. . . .

The term "wedding reception" refers to any type of celebratory function that follows a wedding ceremony, from punch and cookies to a five-course, sit-down dinner. No two functions are alike, because no two couples are alike. Below are general descriptions of some traditional components of a wedding reception that you can adopt, tweak, or jettison in favor of your own ideas and agenda.

ORDER OF EVENTS

The order of events at the reception will vary depending on when photographs of the wedding party are taken, the time it takes to drive from the service to the reception, the type of food service planned, and whether or not there will be music and dancing.

A traditional order of events is:

- arriving guests sign guest book and receive table assignments
- waiters pass beverages and hors d'oeuvres
- wedding party arrives and forms receiving line
- guests go through receiving line
- guests move into dinner or more substantial food is offered at buffets
- orchestra finishes background music and begins dance music

- wedding couple is the first to dance, followed by various family combinations with the couple, and then the dance floor is open to all guests
- toasts are made to the wedding couple
- wedding cake is presented and cut
- bride throws bouquet
- couple departs
- guests begin to depart or remain to dance
- bride's family signals caterer to end beverage service and the band to stop

Any or all of the above can be tweaked to reflect the personal preferences of the wedding couple and their families.

GREETING THE GUESTS

Many couples choose to greet guests individually instead of forming a receiving line that holds them captive for a long period of time. If the number of guests is such that it is possible for the couple to circulate and greet everyone, then a receiving line is unnecessary.

Receiving Lines

Keep the number of members of the receiving line to the absolute minimum. Guests want to see and speak to the newlyweds and their immediate families, not necessarily to the six bridesmaids. Often, the wedding couple's fathers are not included in the line, or they may take turns in the line for short periods of time.

Members of the receiving line should *not* hold glasses or food while in line. The caterer can place a small table behind the line to hold their beverage glasses. Guests going through the line should not have glasses in their hands. They may hold a beverage while waiting but should place their glass on a drop table or hand it to a server before starting through the receiving line.

Order of the Receiving Line

The first person in a receiving line is the host of the event, so the order below would change if the bride's family is not funding the wedding.

- bride's mother
- groom's father (optional)
- groom's mother
- bride's father (optional)
- bride and groom
- matron of honor (optional)
- maid of honor (optional)
- bridesmaids (optional)

The best man and ushers *do not* stand in the receiving line.

Alternatives

Many couples choose to forego a formal receiving line in favor of less restrictive alternatives:

- greeting guests at their tables during the reception
- releasing guests by table at the end of the event
- progressive dance, where the couple dances with as many guests as possible

DINNER SEATING

Consider the information below a snapshot of traditional rules for seating guests at dinner following a wedding ceremony. Couples today have carte blanche to determine how and where they and their guests will be seated.

Bride's Table

- The bride is seated on the groom's right in the center of a long table or round table.
- The best man is seated on the bride's right and the maid or matron of honor on the groom's left (if she is not seated at the parents' table).
- Ushers and bridesmaids fill out the table.
- Place cards are used at the table.

Parents' Table

- The bride's mother has the groom's father on her right and officiant on her left.
- The bride's father is across the table with the groom's mother on his right and matron of honor or other honored female relative or guest on his left.
- Place cards are used at the table.

Sweetheart Table

The wedding couple's role at the reception is to circulate, not to sit at a table for two where they are segregated from their guests. The table serves no purpose.

Guest Seating

- Guests receive table assignments as they enter the reception.
- Tables may be arranged with open seating or by-name seating.

TOASTS

Toasting at weddings used to follow an elaborate protocol:

- best man toasts the bride
- groom toasts the bride
- bride toasts the groom
- father of the bride toasts the couple
- bride toasts the groom's parents
- groom toasts the bride's parents
- matron or maid of honor toasts the couple
- father of the groom toasts the bride
- mother of the bride toasts the couple
- mother of the groom toasts the couple
- other relatives and close friends continue to toast the couple

QUICK TIP
Tacky, Stay Home

Why let any of the following faux pas spoil the tone of your special day?

- **Cake in the Face** Why does anyone think this is a good idea? It's not only messy, it's disrespectful.

- **Best Man's Toast** This is an opportunity to honor the groom and highlight his virtues, not his lapses of judgment. Don't embarrass him or his bride by sharing inappropriate stories. The bachelor party is a better setting for ribbing the groom.

- **Bride's Garter Toss** Three words of advice, keep it classy.

- **Cash Bars** If you can't afford to provide the level of food and beverage that you envision, scale back. Wedding guests should *never* be charged for anything.

We are fortunate that this lineup has been pared down significantly and now, most often, includes:

- best man toasts the couple
- maid or matron of honor toasts the couple
- father of the bride toasts the couple

Some of the missing toasts now take place at the rehearsal dinner.

GIFTS

Gifts are an integral part of weddings. They are meant to convey best wishes for a bright and happy future to the wedding couple. But when givers or receivers spend too much time focusing on dollar value instead of sentiment, the whole process can sour. There are few hard-and-fast rules governing *what* to give, but there are a number of them covering *how* to give and *how* to receive.

GETTING THE WORD OUT

Information on wedding gift registries or gift preferences is never included on a save-the-date announcement or wedding invitation. The save the date may include the address of the wedding website where gift registry information can be found.

Asking for Cash

There are only two permissible methods for a couple to indicate that they prefer to receive gifts of money, and those are by:

Word of Mouth All family members, members of the wedding party, and close friends should be told of the engaged couple's gift wishes so that when others ask for gift advice, they will share the "party line."

Wedding Website Many modern brides and grooms create a website where they share information about prenuptial celebrations, the ceremony, transportation and lodging, and other details that will be helpful to friends and family. The website may include gift registry details or a carefully crafted paragraph regarding the suggestion that money will be appreciated for some practical purpose:

- *We will be married in our hometown and will return to Australia immediately following our honeymoon. We plan to remain there for approximately two years, while we continue to (study/work/snorkel/whatever). Because of the enormous expense of shipping belongings to and from Australia, we do not plan to furnish a home until we return to the States. For this reason, we have not registered for gifts at any of our favorite stores, but we look forward to setting up our home when we return in 2019. For those who may wish to give a wedding gift, we will certainly welcome a contribution to our home-furnishings fund.*

It is *never* OK to ask for money to fund a honeymoon or support wedding or reception costs, but you may make the suggestion of contributions to a favorite charity, if you prefer that to gifts.

Gift Expectations Did you hear the one about the bride with the mistaken notion that the value of each of her wedding gifts should be equal to or exceed the per-person cost of her reception? When some gifts did not equal her calculation, she sent emails to the offending gifters to provide a reception cost rundown and to register her disappointment. Her behavior was not only rude, but greedy and sad as well. The derivation of this misguided gift-value formula is unknown, but let's do our part to disprove it every chance we get.

THANK-YOU NOTES

Attention, grooms. It is the shared responsibility of the wedding couple to write thank-you notes *and to do so immediately after the wedding*. The couple should divide the list, according to their ties to each gift giver, and set deadlines for themselves for completing and mailing the notes. Each note should

- be written within one month (but absolutely no later than three months) following the wedding;
- be handwritten (don't use cards with a preprinted thank-you message);
- include a personalized salutation such as:

    Dear Aunt Mary and Uncle John

    not

    Dear Friends

    or

    To Our Wedding Guests

- mention the specific gift:

    We are thrilled to receive the food processor.

    not

    Thank you for your thoughtful gift.

If the gift was money, it is not necessary to mention the dollar amount in your note, but it personalizes it to mention how you plan to use the money.

QUICK TIP
Gift of Thanks

It is **not acceptable** to email a thank-you note for a wedding gift. Email serves a post-wedding purpose—sharing photos or messages to thank out-of-town guests for coming—but a handwritten thank-you note is a **must** for each wedding gift received or party given in the couple's honor.

Acknowledgments

With gratitude, I acknowledge and thank the following individuals who assisted in the creation of this book:

Jim Mitchell, husband and friend, who for over forty years has supported me with love and kindness and championed my schemes, both harebrained and otherwise;

Patsy Robbins, a loving and loyal sister, whose words and deeds have served as a lifelong example to me of how to treat people with kindness and compassion;

Barbara Coons, Kate Ginman, Dottie Gray, and Kim Moden, who have defined friendship for me for more than thirty years and helped to analyze courtesy conundrums as this book developed;

Victoria Pickering, a strong and steady friend, who for several years served as cheerleader for this project and shared her expertise in social media;

Deb Leopold, a kind friend and leader by good example in the fields of education and social media, who shared her knowledge and insight;

Dr. Sara P. Fogarty, Jean Sperling, Maia Johnston, and Elizabeth Graham, who reviewed material and related experiences and opinions to help develop this book;

Ivor Whitson, agent extraordinaire, who steered me through the labyrinth of book publishing, as he has done for countless others during his long and distinguished career;

And, finally, the Wellfleet Press and Tandem Books teams—John Foster, acquisitions editor, Katherine Furman, editor, Ashley Prine, designer, and Martina Pavlova, illustrator—whose vision, patience, and expertise helped to shape a hazy idea into a book.

Index

Address, forms of, 92–93, 199
Airbnb etiquette, 86–87
Air travel etiquette, 71–75
Appearance. *See* Attire and
  appearance
Art galleries, 63
Attire and appearance
  checklist, attire formality
    definitions, 8–9
  checklist, how clothes should
    fit (by gender and articles of
    clothing), 6–7
  country club guidelines, 65–66
  cruise dress codes, 77
  dress code decoding, 5, 8–9
  dressing to impress, 4
  first impressions, 3, 140
  fitting/fitness of clothes, 4–5,
    6–7
  formal vs. informal attire, 5–9
  hygiene and grooming, 10, 146
  job interviews and, 140–141
  posture, 11
  theater dress code, 61
  value and importance, 3
  workplace dress code, 144
  worship dress code, 58

B&B etiquette, 83–84
Beaches, 64–65
Body language, 23–24, 140–141
Brand (yours), building. *See*
  People skills; Personal best
Buffet etiquette, 185–186
Business cards, 31–32, 149–151,
  154
Busses, tour, etiquette, 76–77

Cards. *See also* Invitations to
  parties, other events; Wedding
  invitations
  business cards, 31–32,
    149–151, 154
  escort cards, 135–136
  place cards, 136–137
Carpool etiquette, 81–82
Cell phone
  courtesy guidelines, 103–105
  cultural experiences and, 62, 63
  dining and, 163, 178, 182
  elevators and, 152
  fitness/fun activities and, 64,
    65, 66, 68

at gym, 68
job interviews and, 140, 142
meetings and, 154–155, 156
parties and, 136
social media and, 108–113, 143
swearing/offensive language
  and, 12
texting, 105, 106–107
travel/transport and, 73, 74, 80
workplace telephone etiquette
  and, 159
Clothing. *See* Attire and
  appearance
Communal living, manners for,
  42–45
Communication, 89–101. *See also*
  Cell phone; People skills; Thank-
  you notes
  body language and, 23–24,
    140–141
  business letters, 90–93
  condolences, 94–97
  email etiquette, 157–158,
    160–161
  forms of address for envelope
    and salutation, 92–93, 199
  grammar importance, 11
  grammar rules review, 97–101
  "No problem" vs. "You're
    welcome," 90
  swearing/offensive language
    and, 11–12
  telephone etiquette, 159
  thank-you notes/letters, 89–90
  when to handwrite, 89–90, 142
Condolences, 94–97
Connecting with others. *See*
  People skills
Cruise etiquette, 77–80
Cup and saucer, 173. *See also*
  Dining etiquette
Curb appeal, of home, 46
Customer, manners as, 51–55
Customer service, 54–55

Deaths, condolences, 94–97
Dining etiquette, 163–188. *See
also* Restaurant dining
  about: overview of, 163
  American style, 174–175
  cup and saucer, 173
  eating and drinking, 165
  ending meal, 166

European style, 176–177
finished position, 175, 177
glassware and, 171–172
napkins and, 169
passing food, 166–167
place settings, 168–173
plate types, 169, 172–173
preparatory steps, 163–165
rest position, 175, 176
salt and pepper, 173
Silent Service Code, 175, 176
SOFT start acronym, 164
soup plate/bowl/cup, 172–173
styles of dining, 173–177
utensils and, 170
wedding reception and,
  205–209
Dinner parties. *See* Parties and
  other social events
Disability etiquette, 37–39
Doctors and medical manners,
  56–57
Dorm life, 43
Dress codes. *See* Attire and
  appearance

Eating out. *See* Restaurant dining
Elevator etiquette, 147, 152
Email etiquette, 157–158,
  160–161
Employee etiquette. *See* Job
  interviews; Workplace manners
Entertainment. *See* Fun and
  fitness
Environment, going green, 49
Environment, your space, 13
Escort cards, 135–136
Etiquette. *See also specific topics*
  rudeness, lack of courtesy
    and, VI
  this book and, VII
  today, perspective on, VI –VII

Facebook, 108–109
Feedback, receiving, 13
First impressions, 3, 140
Fun and fitness, 63–69
  country clubs, 65–66
  gym etiquette, 68–69
  movies, 62
  museums, galleries, etc., 63
  salons and spas, 66–67

swimming pools and beaches,
64–65
theater and performing arts,
61–62

Galleries, art, 63
Gender
courtesies, old school vs. new
school, 148
gender-neutral courtesy,
147–148
transgender courtesy, 34–35
Gifts, general guidelines, 130–131
Gifts, wedding, 209–210
Glassware, 171–172. *See also*
Dining etiquette
Grammar, importance of, 11
Grammar, rules review, 97–101
Greetings and introductions,
24–30
greeting/introducing party
guests, 123–124
handshakes and, 24, 26, 38,
133, 140
introductions guidelines, 25–30
job interview entrance, 140
mastering art of, 24–25
Grooming and hygiene, 10, 146
Gym etiquette, 68–69. *See also*
Fun and fitness

Hair salons, 66–67
Handshakes, 24–25, 26, 38,
133, 140
Health. *See* Fun and fitness;
Medical manners
Historic buildings, 63
Home, manners around. *See*
Living with manners
Hotels and such, 82–87
Airbnb etiquette, 86–87
B&B etiquette, 83–84
hotel how-to/etiquette, 82–83
tipping guidelines, 84, 85, 86
Houseguests, hosts and, 128–129
Hugs and kisses, 24–25
Hygiene and grooming, 10, 146

Image. *See* Personal best
Instagram, 112–113
Interviews, job, 139–143
Introductions, 25–30
Invitations to parties, other events.
See also Wedding invitations
adults-only parties, 120
extending invitation, 115–117

guest list privacy
considerations, 117
online invitations, 116–117
receiving/responding to
invitation, 117–120, 122
rudeness corrective measures,
118–119

Job interviews, 139–143
about: overview of, 139–140
beverages and, 142
body language and, 23–24, 141
cell phones and, 142
departure and follow-up,
142–143
dressing for, 140–141
first impressions, 3, 140
hiring after. *See* Workplace
manners
importance of, 139
name use and recall, 141
seating, table use, and personal
items, 142
thank-you notes, 142–143

Letters. *See* Communication
LinkedIn, 111–112
Listening skills, 19–21, 155
Living with manners
about: overview of, 41
communal living (apartment,
co-op, etc.), 42–45
medical manners, 56–57
move-in ready manners, 41–42
neighborhood watch and, 49–50
neighborliness, 42
parking lots/garages, 59
retail shopping/service
manners, 51–55
roommate rules, 43
in single-family homes, 45–50
worship etiquette, 58–59

Medical manners, 56–57
Meetings, 153–157
Movies, 62
Museums, 63

Name badges, 134–135
Name use and recall, 30–33, 141
Napkins, 169
Neighborliness. *See* Living with
manners
Networking etiquette, 33, 36–37
"No problem" vs. "You're
welcome," 90

Odors and scents, hygiene/
grooming and, 10
Offensive language, 11–12

Parking, courtesy in, 45, 47
Parking lot/garage tips, 59
Parties and other social events
adults-only, 120
aftermath, 124
escort cards, 135–136
extending invitations, 115–117
game plan for, 121
gift guidelines, 130–131
greeting/introducing guests,
123–124
guest considerations, 117, 121
guest guidelines, 125–127
host how-to, 121–125
menu planning, 123
name badges, 134–135
off-site, 125
online invitations, 116–117
party protocol, 131–137
place cards, 136–137
receiving lines, 132–134
receiving/responding to
invitation, 117–120, 122
save-the-date announcements,
118
People skills, 15–39. *See also*
Communication; Greetings and
introductions
about: overview of, 15
body language and, 23–24,
140–141
checklist, dealing with difficult
people, 22
checklist, twelve steps, 16
connecting, building rapport,
17–18
conversational skills, 21
disability etiquette, 37–39
eye contact and, 20, 22, 24, 25,
26, 27, 54
Golden/Platinum Rules, 15
introductions, 25–30
listening skills, 19–21, 155
name use and recall, 30–33, 141
networking etiquette, 33, 36–37
simple gestures, 13
soft skills review, 15–16
transgender courtesy, 34–35
in your neighborhood, 48–49
Personal best. *See also* Attire
and appearance; Greetings and
introductions; People skills

about: preparing for success, 1
building your brand, 2
grammar and, 11, 97–101
hygiene and grooming, 10
job interviews and, 139–143
posture, 11
receiving feedback, 13
swearing/offensive language and, 11–12
timing and punctuality, 12
your space, 13
Pet manners, 49–50
Place cards, 136–137
Place settings, 168–173. See also Dining etiquette
Plate types. See Dining etiquette
Posture, 11
Potluck guidelines, 187–188. See also Buffet etiquette
Public transportation, 80–81. See also Traveling
Punctuality, 12

Rapport. See People skills
Receiving lines, 132–134
Recycling, 49
Religion, worship etiquette, 58–59
Restaurant dining, 177–188
about: overview of, 177
buffet etiquette, 185–186
checklist, management manners, 180
checklist, server misdeeds, 183
checklist, servers' pet peeves, 178
coffee shops, 184–185
customer courtesy, 179–180
drive-through courtesy, 182–184
fast-food guidelines, 182–185
food truck faux pas, 184
kids' table, 180
ordering, 180
potluck guidelines, 187–188
service types (family-style, French, Russian), 188
tapas bar tips, 188
tipping guidelines, 166, 184, 186, 189
Retail, shopping and service manners, 51–55

Sales staff manners, 54–55
Salons and spas, 66–67

Salt and pepper, 173. See also Dining etiquette
Save-the-date announcements, 118, 192, 193–194, 209
Service plate, 169
Shopping, customer and staff manners, 51–55
Snow removal, 47–48
Social media, 108–113, 143
Spas and salons, 66–67
Subway etiquette, 80–81
Success, preparing for, 1. See also Personal best
Swearing, 11–12
Swimming pools, 64–65

Telephone etiquette, 159. See also Cell phone
Texting, 105, 106–107
Thank-you notes
for B&B stays, 84
for condolences, 95, 97
general guidelines, 89–90
for gifts, 118, 124, 131, 211
handwriting, 89–90, 127, 142
helping others with, 95
for houseguest host, 129
for interviewers, post-interview, 142–143
for networking events, 37
for parties, 127
for wedding gifts, 211
Theater and performing arts, 61–62
Timing and punctuality, 12
Tipping guidelines
country clubs, 65, 66
cruises, 80
general guidelines/pointers, 189
hotels/B&Bs/Airbnb, 84, 85, 86
restaurants, 166, 184, 186, 189
salons and spas, 66–67
travel/transport, 76, 77, 80, 84, 85
Toasts, wedding, 208–209
Tours. See Traveling
Train travel, 76. See also Air travel etiquette
Transgender courtesy, 34–35
Trash disposal manners, 46–47
Traveling. See also Hotels and such
air travel etiquette, 71–75
carpool etiquette, 81–82
cruise etiquette, 77–80
subway etiquette, 80–81

tour bus etiquette, 76–77
train travel, 76
Twitter, 110–111, 113

Utensils, dining, 170. See also Dining etiquette

Wedding etiquette, 191–211
about: overview of, 191
ceremony and roles, 204–205
expenses and who pays, 202–203
gifts, 209–210
greeting guests/receiving line, 206–207
planning overview, 191–192
processional/recessional, 204–205
reception and dinner, 205–209
save-the-date announcements, 192, 193–194, 209
thank-you notes, 211
timeline, 192–193
toasts, 208–209
Wedding invitations, 194–208
assembly and mailing, 200
design, 200
forms of address, 199
responding to, 201
text protocol and examples, 194–198
Workplace manners, 139–161
being your best. See Personal best
business cards and, 149–151, 154
customer service, 54–55
dress code, 144
elevator etiquette, 152
email etiquette, 157–158, 160–161
first impressions, 3, 140
gender-neutral courtesy, 147–148
grooming/hygiene violations to avoid, 146
interviews. See Job interviews
medical office/staff, 56–57
meetings, 153–157
new-hire basic tips, 143–146
personal fouls to avoid, 146
sales staff, 54–55
teamwork and, 145
telephone etiquette, 159
Worship etiquette, 58–59

About the Author

Nancy R. Mitchell, The Etiquette Advocate, is an established protocol and etiquette consultant and advisor with more than thirty-five years of experience in the field. Currently, she is an adjunct faculty member at the George Washington University, where she developed and teaches protocol courses in the School of Business. She also teaches them at Stratford University, Falls Church, Virginia.

For twenty-three years, Mitchell was director of Special Events and Public Programs at the Library of Congress, where she coordinated the institution's major special events, visits of heads of state and other foreign dignitaries, fundraising galas, conferences, and meetings. As the library's chief protocol advisor, Mitchell served as liaison to the White House, U.S. Department of State, the Congress, the Supreme Court, and other government agencies, foreign embassies, academia, and corporations.

Mitchell owns and manages the Etiquette Advocate, a firm providing etiquette and protocol training to corporations, nonprofit organizations, government agencies, embassies, universities, the travel and hospitality industry, and individuals. She has been featured on ABC's *Good Morning America*, Fox 5 news, National Public Radio, and WTOP radio; was quoted on matters of etiquette and protocol by CNN, ABC *Nightline*, the *New York Times*, the *Washington Post*, the Associated Press, *Washington Business Journal*, and *Washingtonian* magazine; and has served as an etiquette columnist for Experience.com as well as a technical editor for *Wedding Etiquette for Dummies*. Mitchell is a co-owner and founding partner of the firm Protocol Partners-Washington Center for Protocol Inc.